Digital and Marketing Asset Management

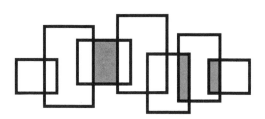

THE REAL STORY ABOUT
DAM TECHNOLOGY AND PRACTICE

Digital Reality Checks is a Rosenfeld Media imprint
developed in partnership with Real Story Group.

 Rosenfeld

Digital and Marketing Asset Management
The Real Story About DAM Technology and Practice
By Theresa Regli

Rosenfeld Media, LLC

457 Third Street, #4R

Brooklyn, New York

11215 USA

On the Web: www.digitalrealitychecks.com

Please send errors to: errata@rosenfeldmedia.com

Publisher: Louis Rosenfeld

Managing Editor: Marta Justak

Developmental Editor: Tony Byrne

Copy Editor: Chuck Hutchinson

Production Editor: Lyza Morss

Interior Layout Tech: Danielle Foster

Cover Design: The Heads of State

Indexer: Sharon Shock

Proofreader: Sue Boshers

ISBN: 1-933820-72-1

ISBN-13: 978-1-933820-72-9

LCCN: 2016939701

Printed and bound in the United States of America

*To Maria Carusi (1957–1999),
who coached me in the art of speechwriting
and public speaking,
and Clif Garboden (1948–2011),
my first boss, who trained me in the craft
of truth-crusading journalism*

*D*igital and Marketing Asset Management: The Real Story About DAM Technology and Practice is based on extensive research involving both vendors who provide DAM technology, as well as the people and organizations that use the technology.

It is an extremely thorough book. And it needs to be. You're going to be making some important decisions on behalf of your department, marketing team, or perhaps your entire enterprise, and my goal is to provide you with as much relevant detail as possible. However, you may not have time to read the book cover-to-cover. Here's a quick guide to maximize the time you spend.

Who Should Read This Book?

Depending on your role in the enterprise, you may want to start at different places in the book and then backfill your knowledge as necessary. Consider the following shortcuts.

- **DAM newbie:** If you're new to DAM and are just looking to get the basics, you should start at the beginning and read the chapters sequentially.

- **Executive sponsor** or **project champion:** Start with Chapter 2, "The Business Case for Digital and Marketing Asset Management," to help distill the business case for a DAM system. You'll also want to explore our discussion of universal scenarios and if you are C-level (or looking to get there soon), be sure to read Chapter 11, "Mixology: DAM in the Digital Marketing Cocktail," as you're likely to play a key role in driving adoption and change management.

- **Project manager:** You might want to begin by getting familiar with the technology through Chapter 4, "DAM Technology Services: Asset Creation and Management."

- **Project engineer:** Refer to Chapters 4 through 7, "DAM Technology Services," to catch up on any key concepts that may be new to you. Then be sure to review Chapter 2, "The Business Case for Digital and Marketing Asset Management," to keep in mind the reasons you're implementing DAM.

- **Consultant/integrator:** How you use this book depends on what you need to provide for your clients. Each chapter can provide useful analysis.

What's in This Book?

The book is broken down as follows:

- **Chapter 1, "What Is Digital and Marketing Asset Management Technology?"** looks at key concepts in digital, marketing, and media asset management.

- **Chapter 2, "The Business Case for Digital and Marketing Asset Management,"** covers the costs as well as the business justification for investing in DAM and MAM.

- **Chapter 3, "The DAM Maturity Model,"** can help you identify how mature your organization's DAM capabilities are across four categories: people, information, systems, and processes. It's also a key piece for justifying further investment in a DAM system.

- **Chapters 4 through 7, "DAM Technology Services,"** explore DAM technology in detail, defining and explaining key features you're likely to find in the technology. Each chapter corresponds to how we break the system features into four main capability areas: "Asset Creation and Management; Search, Retrieval and Navigation; Asset Assembly and Delivery; and Architecture and Administration."

- **Chapter 8, "Cloud, On-Premise, or Hybrid? DAM Delivery Models"** defines the different potential hosting and deployment models for your DAM.

- **Chapter 9, "You're Not Just Buying a Tool: Strategic Considerations,"** examines all the nontechnical considerations you should think about when investing in not just DAM technology, but also the vendor.

- **Chapter 10, "Universal Scenarios: The Key to Comparing Technologies,"** identifies 14 universal DAM scenarios to help you "place" your own needs in the market. They are grouped in four broad categories: image and brand management, publishing, corporate time-based media management, and broadcast media management.

- **Chapter 11, "Mixology: DAM in the Digital Marketing Cocktail,"** looks at where DAM fits in as part of the larger enterprise ecosystem and how to craft the right mix of ingredients for digital marketing success.

What Comes with This Book?

This book's companion website (www.digitalrealitychecks.com/books/digital-and-marketing-asset-management) contains a blog and additional content. The book's diagrams and other illustrations are available under a Creative Commons license (when possible) for you to download and include in your own presentations. You can find these on Flickr at www.flickr.com/photos/rosenfeldmedia/sets/.

CONTENTS

FOREWORD

As a marketing technology professional, I am honored to write the foreword to Theresa's book: it is a great time in the industry for the digital asset management discipline, as DAM has emerged out of the dark basements where arcane taxonomists and unsocial librarians have been cataloging reference images, to finally achieving a prominent place on the center stage of the marketing technology landscape.

Multichannel/multidevice communication, planning, and execution—which is really the only type of communication you should put in place today for your brand—requires near real-time adaptation and distribution of content and its reuse across channels. Of course, many try to go at it with pieces of their content universe distributed across different components of their marketing tech landscape, but the limitations are self-evident: inability to reapply content that works across channels, cul-de-sacs where content is left to "rot," inability to draw conclusions on multichannel performance of the content, manual work and rework to keep systems in sync, just to name a few.

In this context, the smart marketers and technologists who have understood the power of a centralized operational single source of visual records/digital assets use their DAMs in a much-refreshed and strategic way:

1. DAMs that are able via APIs to distribute the assets to the various points of consumer fruition (e.g., a WebCMS, a social publishing solution, an e-commerce mobile application), transforming them as needed, and keeping the cross-references "whole" as much as possible.

2. Tracking performance of assets, going back to the source and the producers for continuous improvement, sometimes using performance-based compensation.

3. Investing in very practical taxonomies, which are not designed for obscure archiving and compliance purposes, but aim to tame the complexity of the outside channels and use cases to maximize automation, increasing findability and introducing efficiencies (content types, channels, content strategies, etc.).

DAMs will also be key for the upcoming wave of intelligent, programmatic content, where we need to be able to rapidly assemble various content constituents to produce original content, to enable a granular personalization for specific consumer segments, in a very specific context.

This book will take you through a journey where you can easily rework your marketing technology strategy and landscape in a more DAM-centric way. It will provide you valuable insights on how to combine marketing technology capabilities in a mix that makes sense for you and your business objectives.

—Filippo Catalano, Chief Digital
Operations Officer, Nestlé

INTRODUCTION

Digital media—photos, audio files, video clips, games, advertising, consumer package designs, streaming television programs, the thousands of music files on your mobile devices—are a significant part of your everyday experience. Both your everyday consumer interactions and the way that organizations market to you are driven by mostly nontextual media. The digital world is more visual, more auditory, and more experiential than it's ever been.

This book is intended for creative media and marketing professionals who know the power of the written word is enhanced and far more effective when accompanied by a commanding image or a piece of moving media. Digital asset management (DAM), the art and science of managing media, marketing, and brand assets, is what makes such experiences possible. Today, DAM is no longer the spotty teenager lurking in the corner of a silo, understood by none other than its contemporaries. DAM is now firmly established as a business-critical application, which is vital in delivering on-brand content to multiple devices and garnering increased user engagement. The imperative to deliver marketing technologies and engaging media at a cloud-enabled scale has resulted in DAM sitting firmly at the feet of the C-suite.

Having long worked in the realm of managing Web content, I was drawn to DAM in 2008, when it seemed clear to me that textual content would soon be eclipsed by online visual media, streaming, and shorter, more marketing-oriented content. I've stayed in DAM for more diverse reasons than that:

- **DAM is a creative pursuit:** More so than the other niches of technology I worked in previously, DAMers are a group of creative, whacky, and truly eccentric people. They run the gamut from representing the realm of artists who want to create beautiful images for nonprofits to marketing professionals who passionately believe in the products and brands they promote.

- **The world needs more DAM:** It's not just big companies that need to manage and deliver media and marketing content effectively; it's also all of us as individuals. I'll never forget one father of five who sent me an email asking for advice: "Two of my kids are off to college, and I want to set up a photo and video sharing system so we can all share our experiences remotely as a family. What would you recommend I use?"

- **DAM enriches our lives:** As a patron of the arts in my hometown of Philadelphia, I have attended the concerts of the Philadelphia Orchestra since my mother took me as a little girl. Today, thanks to DAM, I can read about, listen to, and immerse myself in any piece of music I wish before or after those concerts. Thanks to DAM, a child can have a more interactive educational experience by listening to a poem in the language she's learning. Thanks to DAM, we can watch just about any movie we want whenever we want.

This book will help you understand how you can use DAM for the benefit of your career, yourself, and the organizations you work for.

CHAPTER 1

What Is Digital and Marketing Asset Management Technology?

Since the turn of the millennium, digital media—photos, audio files, video clips, animations, games, interactive ads, streaming movies, and experiential marketing—have become an increasingly significant part of our everyday experience. The combination of inexpensive, highly functional digital still and video cameras (even as part of mobile devices); increased network bandwidth; decreased storage costs; low-cost, high-performance processors; high-capacity, solid-state memory; affordable cloud services; and the requisite digital media infrastructure has laid the foundation for today's vibrant electronic ecosystem. Whether you're browsing the Web, listening to a song on an iPhone, watching a video on a tablet, opening a rich media email on your mobile device, or recording a TV series on a digital video recorder, you're experiencing digital media.

This digital media expansion creates a challenge for consumers and enterprises alike. Consumers want to organize the experience and consumption of digital media files. They want to be able to find them, categorize them, use them when and where they want, and do all this across multiple devices.

Enterprises have a similar but much broader wish list. Of course, they want to be able to find their assets easily—whether for a historical archive or in service of current projects. Most often, they want to use digital media "products" to reach prospective buyers. They may use them as part of a marketing campaign to reach a specific audience in a specific form, such as a brochure, an email promotion, a movie trailer, or a website landing page. The digital media tool also could be the product itself—a music collection, streaming television series, video, electronic magazine, ebook, or catalog—that the enterprise must distribute in a variety of formats or forms.

To produce these products, you need to create, organize, find, and use pieces of digital media: images, graphics, photos, layout and design files, video segments, and audio files. In most cases, you need to add textual information like copy, descriptions, and product data. Finally, you have to put it all together in the right format within the specific production process or workflow. Upon completion, you'll want to distribute and track all the product components, as well as any changes or versions over time. Also, you'll want to know how the various audiences use or consume the product, in both digital and nondigital (for example, paper, CD, and DVD) formats. Additionally (if that were not enough), many digital files have restrictions and rights that must be monitored and respected.

Enterprises have a growing desire to manage the entire lifecycle of digital media. They want to manage each piece of the product independently of, or in addition to, managing the product. This requires a master file that can be transformed into different formats, depending on need and derivative works that are one representation and use of the master.

This management of digital media throughout its lifetime is the general domain of digital asset management (DAM).

Marketing asset management (MAM) often falls under the same rubric, and we'll explore both in the context of DAM. It is against this background that the DAM discussion will begin.

PUNS

Puns on the term *DAM* are, unfortunately, one of the things you will need to get used to if you're pursuing this discipline and technology.

Digital asset management as a discipline and a technology is all about the control, flexibility, portability, access, and reporting of digital assets (images, video, audio, and documents) among organizations, customers, partners, and suppliers. DAM is concerned with delivering the right content to the right people, on all devices (laptops, tablets, TV, and mobile) mostly in real time, with the ability to track and measure digital asset engagement across an enterprise and its potential global reach.

As illustrated in Figure 1.1, digital and marketing asset management is a complex discipline with many moving technological parts, involving not only process and technology but also the people who make the strategy and technology perform. These include a company sponsor, a DAM champion, a librarian (or two), and—most importantly—the stakeholders who will use the system (or not). Whenever possible, you should include those who will use the system to ensure that it meets their needs and that they are comfortable with the new technology. When the different pieces of the technology puzzle come together, it should operate like a humming hive, where the bees have everything they need to produce targeted and personalized digital experiences.

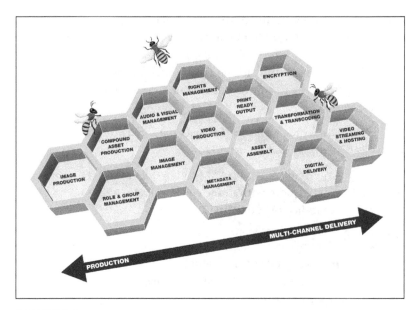

FIGURE 1.1

DAM—and more broadly, creative operations management—is a "hive" of different features and functions spanning production, management, and multichannel delivery.

The origins of digital asset management date back to the early 1990s. DAM's roots lie in image management, publishing, and video (see Figure 1.2). Early DAM vendors attempted to provide a common repository in which to store digital media files. Some vendors started on the desktop, providing a simple database or archive for cataloging and indexing digital images. In many cases, they were cataloging licensed or stock photographs used in brochures or other publications.

Other DAM vendors started in the publishing arena by offering a repository for storing all the files for a particular publishing product, such as a book or magazine. These early functions were dominated by "creatives," who used desktop publishing applications, such as QuarkXPress, Aldus PageMaker (remember those two?), or Adobe's InDesign, and related photo-editing software, such as Adobe Photoshop or Illustrator.

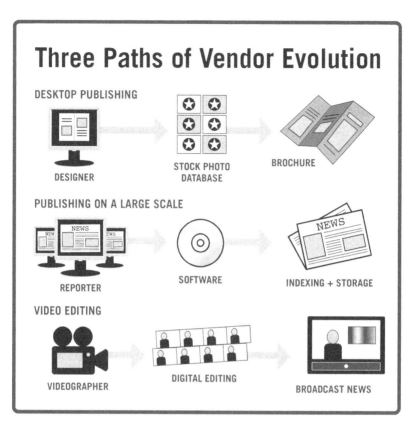

Three Paths of Vendor Evolution

DESKTOP PUBLISHING

DESIGNER

STOCK PHOTO
DATABASE

BROCHURE

PUBLISHING ON A LARGE SCALE

REPORTER

SOFTWARE

INDEXING + STORAGE

VIDEO EDITING

VIDEOGRAPHER

DIGITAL EDITING

BROADCAST NEWS

FIGURE 1.2

Those tools that are now considered DAM tools evolved from three
different origins.

A third group of vendors attempted to support digital video or time-
based asset workflows. At the time, digital video editing was a new
technology. It allowed video editors to cut and paste video digitized
from tape or "ingested" directly from a live broadcast rapidly and
more easily, together with other video, and create entirely new content from the combination. This technology reduced time and cost
while increasing flexibility and creativity. This use of DAM coupled
the DAM repository with the production or broadcast workflow. It
also integrated with pioneering (though proprietary) digital video
editors from companies like Avid and Pinnacle, as well as with VCRs,
playout devices, schedulers, and other broadcast hardware.

This three-pronged origin originally made DAM products fragmented and specialized within the "DAM" umbrella. These lines are blurring as vendors add functionality to reach into areas outside their original domains. Still, DAM products come in many forms, and the most modern waves of new vendors are "born digital"; thus, they are more difficult to wedge into one of the three categories. Some are good at managing particular kinds of media. Others focus on particular use cases, workflows, or processes. The mix of vendors and products you'll find in the marketplace today is varied, with these new "born digital" vendors competing with vendors and products that can trace their roots either directly or indirectly to these first-generation products.

The Blurring of Enterprise Lines

As recently as 2012, it was easy to segment vendors by category, such as "enterprise" or small- to medium-sized workgroup tools. "Enterprise capability" was measured based on scale, integration capability, global footprint, and large clients with global reach. Some of these classifications remain true; however, the advent of the cloud and the breadth of APIs (even among smaller vendors) have blurred the lines between historical "enterprise" vendors and the rest.

Adoption of the gargantuan server farms from the likes of Amazon, Google, Rackspace, and Microsoft (Azure) has been slow but is increasing. Cloud-based pricing from these technology behemoths has kept the landscape competitive, less intimidating, and easier to adopt. Any business can scale rapidly up or down as the need requires in the cloud.

DAM technology is now born in the cloud, or the vendor offers on-premise and cloud-based applications, services, and software-as-a-service (SaaS) environments. Increasingly, cloud-based technology is applied for cold storage archiving. Archives in the cloud would have been unthinkable a few years ago, but tumbling prices and cold storage are bringing archives into real time. A need exists for strong strategies to match, as well as have systems for the full lifecycle of assets, from creation to archive.

This book will deepen your understanding of DAM and help clarify how you will use this technology. We will arm you with the knowledge of how to ask the right questions so that you can create a DAM environment that will achieve your business goals.

The Challenges of Rich Media

Over the past few years, DAM has become an increasingly mainstream and core enterprise application. Conferences, journals, and even informal (but structured) "meet-ups" attest to the growth of DAM. Despite digital asset management being one of the fastest-growing marketing technologies, it may be the least understood.

DAM technology focuses on managing digital, or "rich," media stored in files.

Originally, "rich media" meant anything that wasn't purely text. It also referred to the depth or amount of information contained in the content itself. For example, a video contains visual and oral information; as such, a computer may have difficulty managing the content without human assistance. Examples of rich media include digital forms of images, video, audio, graphics, animations, artwork, games, CAD documents, PowerPoint presentations, or combinations of any of these. Rich media can include created or generated documents (as compared to scanned documents) that are highly structured, have defined page layouts, and contain or reference other content such as images, text, and graphics. These design documents, which may be created in Illustrator, Photoshop, Word, Quark, InDesign, or other programs, are often rendered as PDF files or web pages.

Rich media files pose many challenges:

- **Rich media can be large and unwieldy.** Some video files can be terabytes in size. Print-ready PDF files can be several hundred megabytes. Size affects all aspects of working with the media: storage, processing, movement and distribution, transformation, and search and retrieval. It also affects costs. While network bandwidth continues to increase, moving large files around a network and over geographic distances is still expensive. The most common workaround is to move smaller or lower-resolution representations, or "proxies," thereby reducing cost, increasing speed of access, and facilitating processes that don't need the full, high-resolution form.

- **Rich media is nontextual.** Because it's visual or linear and time-based (such as video), rich media introduces fundamental challenges for how it's identified, presented, searched for, manipulated, transformed, and segmented. Additionally, you may need to determine how to identify, define, and track derivative works. Further, because rich media is nontextual, it requires additional textual information (metadata) describing the media to accompany it either directly, within the repository, or in both places. The need for metadata is essential to DAM, because without metadata, finding your rich media becomes terribly unwieldy to nearly impossible.

- **Rich media requires special handling.** If you work with audio, video, images, and animations, you understand that this media has specialized requirements for manipulation, long-term storage, the kinds of tools or applications you can use with it, and various defining standards. Video has increasingly become a common media type, and it requires a greater technical understanding than other forms of digital media. As a result, it currently has more specialized requirements for its handling, processing, and storage.

- **Rich media is most often managed by a specialized team of people.** Unlike a document management system that nearly everyone within a modern enterprise may use, rich media assets tend to be managed by a specialized team of media specialists. Although marketing and distribution executives may work with everyday software, rich media "creatives" in the trenches work with very specific software, often on a Mac, and bring specialized workflows to the mix.

- **Rich media is growing exponentially.** As the tools for creating and disseminating rich media have become increasingly commonplace and less expensive—notwithstanding the specialized skill sets of many people working with rich media assets—we have seen an explosion in the growth of rich media and the use cases for it. Marketing departments exploit rich media for Web- or Internet-centric campaigns. "How-to" manuals have proliferated. Imagine a time in the not-too-distant future when all car manuals are tablet or small-screen based (in the dashboard). And imagine that these "how-to" manuals are supplemented (or even supplanted) with video tutorials. We are only at the beginning of this process.

- **Rich media represents critical intellectual property (IP).** Pieces of rich media may have intrinsic or explicit value for a company. For example, the copy of a video clip of a CEO interview on CNN may require security, rights, licensing, tracking, and, in publishing scenarios, a way to monetize it. Photographs are also a prime example of rich media as IP with a need to be rights-managed.

Understanding the needs and challenges of rich media files marks the starting point for understanding DAM. There is a difference, however, between a run-of-the-mill rich media file and a "digital asset." This distinction is critical to the definition and essence of DAM.

What Is an Asset?

People often ask, "What are digital assets? And how do we identify ours?" As a starting point, consider the general notion or concept of an *asset: something that has intrinsic or acquired value.* Your house, a building, a coin, a postage stamp, a DVD, a recording, a book, and your skills or abilities are all assets.

Consider an asset conceptually rather than as a physical thing; this may help you understand DAM and its potential usefulness. In theory, a digital asset is *something represented in a digital form that has an intrinsic or acquired value.* This initial definition is intentionally general. It could correspond to almost anything or any piece of media in a digital form, such as a photo, website, or email message.

As a practical matter, however, DAM has evolved to support the management of digital media assets almost exclusively, which includes images, video, audio, and related artifacts (such as brochures and compound publications). You would typically use different types of technology to manage email, Word documents, relational data records, and Web pages.

Even some image "assets" don't fall under the domain of DAM technology as it is known today. Scanned paper or forms that end up as TIFF or PDF files do not constitute media assets that originate through some creative process.

This distinction between rich media and other electronic assets is important because sometimes DAM consultants or vendors will suggest that DAM tools are suitable for managing *all* of your electronic assets, when in fact, they are not. While this is less common than in the earlier days of DAM, be on guard against this false assertion.

Therefore, we refine our working definition a bit: *A digital asset corresponds to a media file or files that have an intrinsic or acquired value.* For example, a movie, television show, magazine, or book has an implicit intrinsic value that today is increasingly produced digitally. These types of assets tend to be easier to understand, since they are both digital assets and "the products" being manufactured for sale. They have (in a manner of speaking) "shareholder" value. By contrast, a brochure, white paper, or banner advertisement may also have brand equity and marketing value, but no value as a direct income-generating asset. An asset's value may fluctuate over time. The key factors for DAM are that the asset has some value throughout its lifetime and that someone wants to use or reuse the asset. A discussion in Chapter 2, "The Business Case for Digital and Marketing Asset Management," will introduce some considerations and best practices for identifying the digital assets you want to retain.

CAVEAT

This definition also allows for physical objects such as DVDs, videotapes, film reels, product samples, film costumes, and museum items to be included as "assets." While this may appear to be a stretch, consider enterprises that need to catalog physical items and provide a digital form or proxy to represent them, such as a museum cataloging its collection of Renaissance paintings. Now you have a digital image or icon representing the physical thing, so the definition of a digital asset actually includes both digital and physical things.

Metadata

We have not yet reached a final definition. Technically speaking, a digital asset is more than just the media file. To realize the value of that file (or collection of files), you need to have additional information about that asset. In short, you need "metadata." For most DAM purposes, we define *an asset as the media content itself, plus its metadata* (see Figure 1.3). Metadata can be as simple as the name, author, or creation date of the file or as complex as the rights and fees around use of an image or the extracted speech converted to text from a video.

The three fundamental types of metadata are as follows:

- **Implicit:** It's an inherent part of the asset, such as date created, file size, MIME type, date modified, author ID, and so forth. It's called "implicit" because a human being did not decide those values. The values are inferred from the file's physical characteristics.

- **Explicit:** A human or an automated process made some judgments about the asset, such as subject, ranking, category, or value, or manually overwrote an implicit value, such as changing the author.

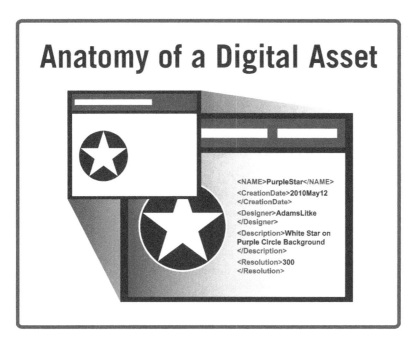

FIGURE 1.3
Content becomes an asset when metadata is associated with it.

- **Derived:** The metadata is extracted from an asset, such as text extracted from a PowerPoint file and made searchable, or text pulled automatically from another system and applied to the file. Derived metadata often constitutes a first-class content asset in its own right and may have metadata of its own.

CAVEAT

In a DAM system, metadata can be physically bound to (embedded in) the asset itself or stored separately—typically in a database. We get into this distinction later, but for now, don't get confused between how the metadata is linked to an asset and the logical types of metadata we've described. Implicit does not mean embedded, and vice versa.

Metadata is essential to managing assets. Metadata provides useful information about the content, such as "Older woman holding a baby" photo, taken by Phil Smith, on January 5, 2008 (see an actual example in Figure 1.4). It makes content accessible and searchable, provides context, defines usage rights, shows an asset's history of use, and, over time, can be used to determine an asset's value.

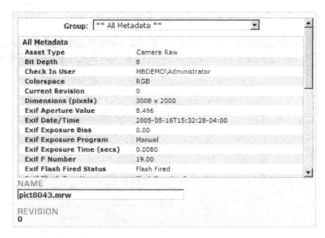

FIGURE 1.4

Implicit metadata for a photo taken with a digital camera.

Metadata can, in a sense, become an asset itself. It is invaluable, and you will need to manage it as well.

There are many different categories of metadata. In fact, your choice of fields here is endless. In the sections on DAM Services (Management Services) and Standards (Dublin Core) in Chapter 7, "Dam Technology Services: Architecture and Administration," we talk more about metadata and discuss the categories that tend to matter most for digital asset management.

To sum up, here is the complete definition of a digital asset in the DAM context:

> A digital media file or collection of files, consisting of the content itself plus metadata, which together have an intrinsic or acquired value, and represent a digital or physical entity.

If, however, you find this definition too conceptual, just think of digital assets as the media file plus its metadata.

Digital and Marketing Asset Management Defined

In its simplest form, a digital asset management system provides a secure repository that facilitates the creation, management, organization, production, distribution, and, potentially, monetization of media files identified as digital assets.

Like other content management technologies, DAM provides basic library services: a common (typically centralized) and secure place to store, organize, and retrieve files. It is also core process services, including specific facilities for the management, manipulation, transformation, security, movement, and processing of rich media files and their metadata. Most DAM systems can now integrate with other tools and systems.

Integration into creation and publishing tools and with other systems is an important question in product selection. Content management vendors often tout their tools' ability to "manage" rich media. Specifically, they offer repositories that can store and control binary files and apply access rights and workflows to those files. In some cases, they provide some basic image manipulation services. We call this "DAM Light," and for many enterprise scenarios, it may suffice. For the more sophisticated scenarios of the kind we identify in the Publishing and Video Production domains of Chapter 10, "Universal Scenarios: The Key to Comparing Technologies," you need a full-blown DAM system, which provides a particular set of unique services.

DAM tools support specialized types of content, which have needs that web content management (WCM) and document management (DM) systems can't meet. Specialized DAM teams within the enterprise employ highly specialized collateral tools to prep and distribute that content.

Key functional differences also exist. DM tools tend to emphasize either simple Office document collaboration or the processing of large volumes of scanned images. WCM tools manage websites and associated content, although only the Web form of that content.

In contrast, DAM technology manages a master file or asset expressed in multiple digital or physical forms. For example, an image stored in the DAM system would have multiple different renditions, such as different approved sizes, formats, scales, coloring, or alterations, each depending on its use, such as for the Web, print, or banner ads. As such, the DAM could actually feed content to the WCM or WCM repository in an appropriate form.

Functionally, DAM systems have several capabilities not found in other types of content management systems:

- **Direct ingestion services:** The ability to ingest or migrate large amounts and various types of assets directly into the system, without one-by-one, manual insertion.

- **Transformation, transcoding, and extraction:** The ability to render assets in different formats, sizes, scales, file types, or resolutions, or change the audio and video characteristics, encoding, or bit rate of the asset, respectively.

- **Rendition management:** The ability to manage multiple, individual renditions of an asset, such as a preview, a proxy, one for the website, and one for print, and of each version of that asset. Thus, if the asset itself is changed or versioned, its related renditions act as an organic function of the DAM software and of asset management in general. Every asset will always have additional renditions of itself that are automatically generated and are related to it.

- **Rights and intellectual property management:** The ability to manage, distribute, and reuse assets based on the IP rights the organization has around the asset.

DAM Technology Services

While digital and marketing asset management products don't vary much in terms of what they can do, they do vary wildly in *how* they do it from an architectural and user experience perspective. Every DAM tool has certain common services and functionality and also some that may be unique, additional, or particular to a specific product or industry application or a use case.

As you get further into the book, we'll dive deeper into DAM technology:

- The components of and services performed by a DAM system

- The overall technology and architecture of these systems and the implication of architectural choices on function and services

- Some general platform capabilities and features

If you look at DAM systems from a mechanical perspective, it's about process management on top of information architecture. In fact,

DAM technology provides several layers of services. The key question for your enterprise is "How can the system's features help or hinder you and your team in achieving your business requirements around creation, management, assembly, and distribution of digital and marketing assets?"

We use a couple of different perspectives to examine an asset management system. The first is a comparative logical versus physical view. The logical view describes the set of functions it performs and the services it provides. This view doesn't necessarily describe how the system performs the function or where in the system it performs that function.

In contrast, the physical view shows you the system architecture, laid out onto tiers with actual hardware and software. Two different products or implementations could provide very similar sets of services, yet have different architecture. This comparison can lead into a completely different set of questions and understanding about the scalability, throughput, capacity, distribution, and reliability based on the system's architecture.

In general, DAM systems perform and provide a broad range of functions. Vendors typically cluster these functions into four areas: create, manage, deliver, and administer. But let's start at the beginning, the features and functions that make a DAM system what it is.

Ten Core Characteristics of a DAM System

In a partnership with the DAM Foundation (**www.damfoundation.org**), Real Story Group and other industry experts have created a set of functional requirements that define a true DAM. This is now ratified as an industry standard. Together, we have developed a testing methodology to judge vendors as part of our ongoing research. The 10 core criteria follow:

- Ingest
- Secure
- Store
- Transform
- Enrich

- Relate
- Process
- Find
- Preview
- Produce/Publish

1. Ingest

DAM systems *ingest* assets individually or in mass sets, and allow for the manipulation of those assets and their metadata individually or with mass actions.

The vendor must

- Demonstrate that there are different methods by which assets and metadata can be uploaded to the DAM.

- Demonstrate embedded metadata writing and extraction.

- Demonstrate bulk or batch actions and ingestion workflows.

2. Secure

DAM systems *secure* the assets they contain. Security in a DAM system extends to defining access control lists (ACLs) for assets and defining roles for users accessing the system.

The vendor must

- Demonstrate methods by which different users or user groups can be given differing levels of capability to perform actions on the DAM.

- Demonstrate that administrators are able to add new users and non-named users securely or that they have facility for SSO.

- Demonstrate that rights can be managed via embedded metadata, notifications, and expiration dates.

3. Store

DAM systems *store* assets as both binaries and metadata. A DAM system can store multiple file types and allow for the customization of metadata fields. The metadata in those fields can then be attached to the stored files.

The vendor must

- Demonstrate that a range of asset types can be ingested and supported by the DAM.

- Demonstrate that users are able to use metadata to turn content into assets via various means.

4. Transform

DAM systems *render* or *transform* assets on ingest into new forms, such as thumbnails or proxy files. The new forms generated on asset ingest via transformation should all be stored as asset parts of the original file. Transformation can also occur when a user downloads files from the DAM system later or during automatic distribution.

The vendor must

- Demonstrate thumbnail and proxy creation.

- Demonstrate some capacity for asset editing such as cropping.

- Demonstrate that either multiple transcodes or transformations are produced on ingest or can be requested on download.

5. Enrich

DAM systems *enrich* assets through the application of metadata and metrics during the use and reuse of an asset throughout its lifecycle.

The vendor must

- Demonstrate that global data is held on site usage (downloads, traffic, and so on) and preferably holds data on assets and individual users as well.

- Demonstrate that this data is available for download and prefer-ably that this data can be used to create reports, graphs, and tables on the DAM or by using a third-party integration.

6. Relate

DAM systems *relate* assets by tracking the relationships between and among an original asset and versions or variants of the original. Versioning and version control tools are central to an asset's life in a DAM system.

The vendor must

- Demonstrate that assets can be saved as versions, accessible from the asset, which can be viewed and reinstated.

- Demonstrate other ways that relationships can be created between assets.

- Demonstrate that UIDs are in use and how different versions are linked via these IDs.

7. Process

DAM systems regulate a structured *process* in the management, creation, and review of assets with workflow tools. Via programmed workflows, DAM systems allow a decentralized workforce to collaborate in a centralized system.

The vendor must

- Demonstrate that there are ways that processes can be streamlined, using ingestion or review and approval workflows, for example, but preferably with multiple workflow options.

- Demonstrate ways that workflows can be tracked, regulated, and assigned to different users (at minimum, emailing notifications to users).

8. Find

DAM systems enable users to *find* assets and retrieve those assets by facilitating search through metadata, collections, workflows, and access control tools. By increasing the discovery of assets that may not have been easily accessible before ingestion, a DAM system assists workers in leveraging existing content for maximum potential.

The vendor must

- Demonstrate that all metadata can be searched and can perform advanced searches with AND/OR search queries (for example, using Boolean logic).

- Demonstrate that there are multiple ways to organize assets and then navigate through the system. Taxonomies, lightboxes, and saved searches are examples of features that aid navigation.

9. Preview

DAM systems have a *preview* function that allows users to view assets before downloading or opening files on their devices. Because the preview feature searches quickly—without download—DAM systems reduce users' search time.

The vendor must

- Demonstrate that images, documents, and audiovisual assets can be previewed in the DAM system.

- Demonstrate that batches of assets can be grouped into lightboxes or presentation areas that can be shared internally and externally.

10. Produce/Publish

DAM systems *produce* or *publish* content by distributing assets outside the system by sharing, linking, and more. This DAM function may be as simple as generating a URL on ingest or as complex as allowing users to build collections of items for sharing with a workgroup.

The vendor must

- Demonstrate that there are facilities by which assets can be published or content using assets can be produced on the DAM system or via an integration or plug-in.

- Demonstrate that assets can be published using embeds, unique links, or similar.

In general, DAM systems help companies manage their digital media at various points throughout the lifecycle of the media and lifetime of the business. They aim to facilitate workflows that involve this media—whether they're creative, production, or distribution workflows—or broader business processes, like video or advertising production, marketing campaign management, or marketing collateral distribution.

The Rise of Lightweight DAM Offerings

In its early days, digital asset management was simply about storing, organizing, and retrieving digital content. Now DAM does much more than that, but for those whose needs are basic, simpler functionality may be adequate. Today, some products on the market fill the niche of "DAM Light" and are at the lower end of the price scale. While they may not meet all 10 core characteristics of a DAM, they are a significant step up from a shared drive.

Many of these less specialized DAMs are "born digital," and are fully Web-based, which allows for straightforward setup and installation. Generally, costs are low. However, be aware that these are closer to iPhoto or Box.com on steroids than they are to a true DAM, per the 10 core characteristics listed previously.

A number of established vendors offer a "slimmed-down" version of their DAM product, where it's possible to carry out basic actions (upload, download, search, and share). Given the vast array of choices in this market, it's easy to see why some of the bigger vendors are tapping into this niche. For you, there's an added benefit, since you can easily upgrade to the full product after you've determined that the simple version is effective in your company.

Some vendors sell different modules or feature packages that can be bolted on to the "Light" version when needs dictate:

- Version control
- Editing and rendering
- Transformation and transcoding
- Document support
- Workflow
- Plug-ins and integrations

CHAPTER 2

The Business Case for Digital and Marketing Asset Management

Demand continues to accelerate within enterprises to manage digital media assets. Managing rich media files is no longer a "nice-to-have" but a "must-have" in marketing groups, IT organizations, and media/entertainment operations groups. The rapid growth of digital media and the recognition of the need to manage it, however, often catch many enterprises by surprise. Enterprises tend to have a limited understanding of just how poorly managed their digital media is and of all the work involved in producing, maintaining, or delivering their digital media products or artifacts.

For most enterprises, the middle managers (many times these are marketing managers) that sit between the "creatives" and upper management may have the greatest sense of the problems that their teams encounter with digital media. At a senior management level, most organizations lack the appreciation, understanding, or perspective for the severity of the problem. They don't recognize its impact on the business and the value that DAM technology can provide.

Of course, a DAM tool alone will not yield all of the benefits we've outlined. Here, we'll identify some of the process changes and other practices required to achieve these benefits. Nevertheless, while DAM technology alone may not suffice for better media management, it is certainly necessary.

Exploiting the Who, What, When, and Where of Digital and Marketing Assets

To understand the value and be able to articulate and provide a strong business case to your manager, you have to understand the problem facing your enterprise. Most enterprises don't know the answers to these statements:

- What digital media they have.
- Where it is.
- How to find it.
- What form it's in.
- What rights they have to it.
- How to locate it and get it delivered in the form they need when they need it.

- How to publish it in multiple forms to different channels, often simultaneously.

- The costs involved for all of the above.

If any of this rings true for you, you're not alone. The problems companies face in dealing with digital media are much more common than you might think:

- Someone can't find an image, video, or a piece of media that someone else needs *right now.*

- The production or distribution process—or some large part of it—isn't streamlined.

- Too many silos of media or disconnected systems don't work together.

- The amount and kind of storage required for video—especially high-definition (HD) video—is lacking.

- Multiple systems duplicate or complicate efforts.

- Multiple efforts focus disconnectedly on pieces or on similar things in multiple noncommunicating groups across the organization.

- Media can't easily be shared across projects, groups, divisions, partners, or distribution mediums.

- The collaboration, review, and approval cycle is slow, inefficient, and manual. The material isn't in a form that everyone can review, especially partners or legal reviewers outside the company.

- People are always re-creating content, artwork, layouts, slides, presentations, and assets—starting from scratch every time.

- You find it difficult or impossible to reuse your own or other people's work.

- Your team can't respond rapidly or at all to partners, customers, or clients.

- Your boss wants to make money off the assets but can't.

- Tracking revisions of works in progress or finished works is difficult, or you can't track asset use—where it's used, who is using it, and how frequently it's used.

- Confusion reigns around the (manual) tracking of licensed photos, images, or other assets.

- The marketing message isn't presented consistently across groups, organizations, verticals, and target markets.

- Your logo is misused, or your brand is inconsistently used.

- Your FedEx or UPS account has recurring invoices for shipping DVDs "urgently."

- A group was fined for violating the usage rights of a licensed photo because no one knew the rights—which weren't with the image, and couldn't be looked up easily.

If your office has faced any of these challenges, you're on your way to identifying where a DAM system could bring value to your organization.

Supporting Strategic Organizational Initiatives

We've seen three major rationales for investing in a DAM tool. At a high level, enterprises face pressure to do the following:

- Reduce costs.

- Generate new revenue opportunities.

- Improve market or brand perception and competitiveness.

Cost reduction implies greater operational efficiency. You do more with what you have, do the same or more with less than what you have, or wring out costs by optimizing or changing processes. Greater operational efficiency entails increased communication and collaboration; automation; and sharing of resources, systems, and processes.

New revenue generation requires developing new products or services, finding new or expanded uses for existing products and services, or uncovering new or adjacent markets for existing products. At the core, this process requires operational agility. The organization must have the internal drive and collaboration to change processes and make things happen; the infrastructure must facilitate a quick response to new opportunities.

Even if your new products and services are not digital (most are not), your enterprise needs to produce, manage, and deliver an increasingly broad set of collateral information for each new or revised offering. Today, much of that collateral consists of rich media (videos, podcasts, images, and the like). In other words, your digital and marketing assets need to evolve and adapt as fast as your revenue streams, and that takes proactive management.

While *improving market or brand perception and competitiveness* is primarily a marketing function, other groups, including sales, service, and support, and in some cases research and development (R&D) or engineering, play a role. These groups share three goals:

- Improve responsiveness to customer needs and market demands and accelerate time to market—often with fewer resources.

- Increase the consistency of the brand and marketing message across the organization, sales channels, media, and various customer interaction points.

- Increase the company's competitive position by improving the perception of the brand, the product, and the organization itself.

Asset management systems contribute and support these high-level business goals through DAM-centric initiatives. These initiatives may be strategic or tactical and may be focused entirely within the marketing group or may span groups, divisions, or extended constituencies within and beyond company walls (for example, partners or ad agencies). Frequently, they start within one group and expand deliberately or opportunistically to others over time. This growth, if not managed thoughtfully, can bring with it a separate set of organizational issues. For example, seasoned DAM users from marketing could end up with phone calls and emails from a department that is new to asset management. You should almost expect this to happen in a maturing DAM environment, so plan accordingly.

A DAM system provides a centralized and secure repository for media assets. In and of itself, this can enable cost reduction and containment in several forms:

- It reduces or eliminates hard costs by

  - Eliminating the production, duplication, and shipping costs of physical media, such as videotapes, CDs, or DVDs.

  - Introducing a common architecture and infrastructure shared by multiple groups, potentially eliminating or consolidating multiple disparate existing systems, thereby reducing ongoing maintenance and support costs.

- Creating process efficiencies by establishing a core shared services infrastructure and streamlining content-centric business processes. Broadcast, media, and entertainment industries have embraced this trend as they move from analog and digital workflows to file-based workflows. The print and publishing industries are only now beginning to grapple with multichannel publishing and end-to-end, file-based digital workflows.

- It reduces or eliminates soft costs (such as workflow-related costs) by

  - Optimizing workflows around a shared repository and shared assets.

  - Reducing or eliminating content or asset location costs (making assets easier and quicker to find).

  - Reducing and/or eliminating recreation costs.

  - Increasing asset reuse.

  - Enabling asset sharing across and between organizations both locally and globally.

  - Enabling multiple distribution mediums.

  - Creating new, streamlined, lower-cost, and file-based workflows (for example, reduced routing/approval cycles).

  - Reducing employee, partner, and customer frustrations around poor search capability for your existing assets.

Never underestimate the impact of these frustrations as brakes on productivity.

> **CAVEAT**
>
> Soft costs can be difficult to calculate because most enterprises have not measured them. Enterprises typically don't have an accurate understanding of the costs or metrics of the "before" scenario—how you did things before you used an asset management system—to compare to the actual cost benefits or metrics from the "after-installation" scenario. Still, it may be empirically obvious that your enterprise can now do things that it just couldn't do before or appears to be doing certain processes faster or more efficiently. For instance, you are creating more material of higher quality, with the same number of people, or you are adding more value to the organization with fewer people.

Improving Collaboration and Streamlined Creative Workflow

DAM technology can improve the overall creative, production, storage, and distribution efficiencies of an organization with respect to rich media workflows. A DAM system and its related file-based workflows can enhance your revenue generation by speeding time to market for new products because you can shorten the creation cycle of essential marketing materials. DAM systems can rapidly improve joint-venture collaboration between marketing teams, brands, and agencies by allowing teams to both share and collaborate around a set of assets, and literally see what they have to work with. In addition, seeing and envisioning a specific asset in some future use or campaign can spur new ideas.

DAM technology can enable new business and revenue opportunities by allowing organizations to enter new markets with digital products because they can produce and distribute them more quickly than by using prior approaches. For example, a firm may migrate movies rapidly from theatrical release to online or DVD distribution, or be able to publish the same photographs and copy in multiple books with slightly different target audiences. In many traditional verticals (such as manufacturing and financial services), DAM systems enable companies to rapidly open and support new distribution channels with consistent materials. Marketing teams can adapt more quickly to emerging opportunities by reusing materials, metadata, and access protocols. In addition, these channels can create a competitive advantage, allowing the organization to be more adaptive, responsive, and agile.

Developing Better Brand Management

Your marketing organization can improve its brand and market perception and competitiveness using DAM technology. It allows marketing groups to better enforce and monitor brand usage and consistency because everyone from internal marketing operations people to field sales to account reps use the same approved digital media in the right formats.

DAM technology can support rights-managed asset tracking to ensure compliance and the proper use of photographs and other licensed digital materials. In advertising, your field and brand marketers and agency partners can more easily support style guidelines and brand usage. You can rapidly create localized marketing materials using existing brand assets in approved publishing templates and formats. Distributors and field sales representatives can be sure they have only the most recent and approved brand assets or product information.

Enabling Marketing Agility and Operational Excellence

Because the marketing organization within the enterprise typically uses the DAM system, its value propositions tend to be more marketing-specific. Overall, a DAM system can play a critical role in improving marketing agility and operational excellence. From the perspective of a VP of Marketing or Chief Marketing Officer (CMO), a DAM system can provide significant value in addition to the aforementioned improved collaboration, workflow, and brand management:

- **Risk mitigation:** A digital and marketing asset management system ensures that you use rights-managed and licensed brand assets in compliance with contractual terms.

- **Accountability:** A DAM gives CEOs and other executives better metrics on creative spending by providing measurable reporting on the worldwide use and cost of brand assets.

- **Investment optimization:** With a single "gold master" system centralizing and automating the delivery and use of brand assets, CMOs can track asset use and better optimize investments in brand assets through greater asset reuse.

- **System justification and expansion:** A DAM system tracks its use within the enterprise, so the CMO can monitor adoption, expansion, and resistance. Critical usage metrics, such as who is using the system the most, how often, and who isn't, provide valuable information for annual budgeting and expansion planning. If you can document increasing adoption and use, you're more likely to get annual budget increases to expand the system further throughout the enterprise. You can use this data as a political whip, prod, or embarrassment to get noncompliant groups on board, thereby increasing not only adoption but also brand compliance and investment optimization.

- **A revenue center:** In larger product companies and in all sizes of services organizations, a DAM system serves as an internal paid-for brand management or marketing service to internal constituencies, such as brand managers, regional sales or marketing teams, and regional field reps. Services organizations—such as advertising agencies, printers, service bureaus, and video production houses that offer DAM as an add-on service to their clients—have adopted similar approaches.

You don't need to examine *all* of these potential benefits in the context of your particular situation, and you should not assume that you would immediately reap such a wide array of rewards. Instead, determine which potential benefits would be most significant to you and your organization and weigh them against the potential costs of implementing a specific DAM solution. You can then map your goals to the appropriate scenario and, in turn, to the most appropriate tool for *you*.

Examining DAM Costs

DAM deployments incur a variety of different costs. The software fees are dwarfed by all of the other components of the system. The primary cost categories are as follows:

- Software
- Hardware and storage
- Networking
- Metadata and taxonomy development
- Consulting, configuration, and customization
- Integration with other systems
- Related applications and services
- Support
- Training
- Ongoing operations
- Adjustment costs
- Content costs

As with other content technologies, DAM project managers and sponsors face the immediate challenge of allocating costs appropriately. For example, DAM deployments commonly require integration into additional broadcast-specific systems, as well as other enterprise software such as the WCM, identity management, or authentication services (such as LDAP or Microsoft's Active Directory), ERP, intranet, or billing systems. Be sure to consider all of these costs when you determine your budget for a DAM system. In other cases, if the DAM system should be accessible to business partners outside the company firewall, you may require additional network security. How an enterprise allocates these costs depends largely on organizational and political influences.

Before we jump into specific costs, let's look at "scale." In general, your costs will depend on the scale of your system. Scale derives from several factors, but primarily it boils down to the number of users—both total users and those concurrently accessing the system. In some cases, scale will refer to geographic size, with multiple instances of the software or hardware residing in geographically dispersed locations. Scale will contribute to the cost of both software and hardware. Vendors or market analysts often describe scale in terms of the breadth of usage in enterprise, department, and workgroup sizes.

The term *enterprise*, in particular, may have different meanings to different vendors. It may refer to instances in which DAM system use cuts across two or more departments; DAM systems have custom integration with other software systems in the organization; or either a large number of users across the enterprise use the system, or a large number of users—many of whom reside outside the company—use the system.

The majority of DAM deployments up until about 2014 were departmental in size—less than a few hundred users. These deployments, however, may have users from multiple departments and from outside the company, such as ad agencies or printers. When considering scale, understand what *you* mean by scale. Moreover, when vendors brag about—or reference—a specific "large-scale" customer, ask what *they* mean by the scale of that customer's deployment. Many of the initial implementations are evolving from departmental to more centralized systems. If this describes your situation, ask your vendor for specific case studies and the ups and downs of "scaling."

Now, let's dig into the major cost categories.

Software

Like all software suppliers, DAM vendors across the marketplace offer a variety of licensing models to try to fit the needs of the customer and create a predictable revenue stream for themselves.

In the past, perpetual licenses were common. In recent years, term licenses have become more popular, as have software-as-a-service (SaaS) models, in which the vendor provides the software as a hosted service and the client essentially leases it. Some of the hosted/SaaS vendors also function as managed service providers (MSPs), in which you purchase the software and own the license, and they host it for you on either your or their hardware.

DAM software licenses—whether installed or hosted—typically use one of the following licensing/pricing approaches:

- **Per CPU:** This approach is common for installed software, typically for server-side components, though it is sometimes coupled with per-user pricing for various client-side or add-on components. The per-CPU model changes dramatically when you look at cloud-based provisioning. With this model, you pay only for the CPU you use at any given time. An example is a video that goes viral; you want enough computing power to deliver the experience to all of your users. In the cloud model, you pay only for the extra CPUs used during the time the video spikes, and they tail off as the spike declines along with the pricing associated with it. You rent what is used and pay nothing if it is not used. Be aware that in a locally installed, licensed system, server upgrades lead to additional expenses. Some distinction may be made for server-side software used for deployment versus that which is used for development or staging.

- **Per user:** This approach is typically categorized into different types of users, based on levels of use, or access to a defined set of functions or capabilities at different price points. This model is used for both installed software as well as for cloud/SaaS. Vendors have several variations of this pricing model:

  - **Named user:** This model specifies a specific, identified user.

  - **Concurrent user:** Sometimes referred to as a *floating license*, this model specifies a fixed number of pooled licenses to be used on a first-come/first-served basis.

- **Power user:** This model specifies a user who has access to all system functions, akin to an administrative license.

- **Casual user:** This model offers limited capabilities, usually restricted to search, read, and download.

- **Any combination of the above:** Using this approach, all users need to be identified, but the licensing is typically based on a maximum number of concurrent users.

- **By volume:** As cloud solutions become the new normal, many vendors base their pricing on the amount of storage space you use, as well as the spiking CPU data mentioned earlier. The more CPU and RAM used, or the more cloud servers are used, the higher the price. When the processing power is not used, pricing reverts back to the user-seat or per terabyte model. Some vendors charge more for power users, such as administrators who set up the system, and some base their pricing on the concurrent number of users. The main benefit of the latter approach is that you will always scale based on users' needs, with no significant drop in service for one to one million users.

As a cautionary note, the very nature of viral video is the difficulty in predicting it. You should budget in the event of a massive viral video hit and have a strategy in place as part of your governance policy.

Other considerations with respect to user numbers and the use of high-resolution images and videos include the bandwidth available at your offices. If a small pipe connects you to access in a cloud-based environment, you need a strategy regarding whether high-resolution images and video should be used and, if so, when and how.

Some vendors mitigate this problem by using for position only (FPO) images in software design programs like InDesign. A smaller resolution image is used in place of the high resolution, and when the work is complete (such as a printed catalog), the system matches the high-resolution image to the FPO, thus mitigating bandwidth issues. Others lock out the high-res images from the system. This approach still relies on bandwidth since it must be downloaded and then uploaded. Further, it can lead to many asset versions. Plan accordingly.

A Special Note on Open Source

Many people believe that software should be free and that collaborative efforts should be made to improve the software to everyone's benefit. Even commercial DAM products are littered with open source components, and many DAM systems run on Linux, perhaps the most well-known open source initiative out there. Most DAMs use Lucene, Solr, or (increasingly) Elasticsearch as their search engine, which is another example of how deeply open source is interwoven with DAM.

A number of open source vendors also are becoming more prominent in the market. While the software is free, vendors will generally recoup what they lose in software licenses by offering professional services and hosting. As with on-premise implementations, open source platforms incur IT costs, and depending on the level to which you hope to customize the DAM, a level of development knowledge is also necessary.

There is variability in open source provisions, and a lot of this relates to the type of software license under which the initiative operates. The main differentiator is whether or not developers are obliged to share the components they develop for their system with the community. In both cases, the success of the open source platform relies on a community of developers who build out on the system. When obliged to share their developments, adopters of the system automatically become contributors. However, when not obliged, adopters usually rely on the original development team or on hosting providers that have adopted the system for their own means and built on it.

While open source aims to give control back to you, as the implementer, effectively enabling you to become the master of your own destiny rather than relying on the success (or failure) of a chosen DAM provider, don't be fooled into thinking it will be simpler or less expensive than a licensed software package. It often is not.

In general, a per-user license allows you to buy what you need, which can be particularly useful in early stages of DAM deployments when adoption is uncertain, or the number of specific users is limited, as in a phased rollout. This method, however, becomes more expensive as the number of users increases, and is falling out of fashion as more vendors move toward an instance-based licensing model. If your pricing is user-based, be sure to ask how the "users" are counted because some DAM vendors include Web-based access from external third parties as one "user" (or an unlimited user group with a single price), and others may count each person at an external agency as a user. The differences can add up and are important considerations for careful license costing.

To the extent that most systems will scale to a specific number of users per CPU, you can compare this approach to per-CPU pricing in your calculations. Of course, some DAM services and products are more processor-intensive than others are, so you'll want to test your calculations carefully before final budgeting.

- **Per module:** As with most enterprise software, DAM vendors sell optional modules or components that provide discrete sets of functions.

- **Per asset:** A few DAM vendors license their software based on the maximum number of assets expected to be stored in the system. They base the pricing on the scale of the repository from an asset—not user—perspective. Vendors sometimes couple this approach with per-user or per-component/module approaches.

- **Enterprise license:** For large deployments, vendors employ an "enterprise" license, which provides both unlimited seats and "all you can eat" in terms of optional modules. These licenses aren't on the standard price list and are typically negotiated individually.

As you can see, pricing models vary dramatically. During your evaluation process, you need to understand how your prospective vendors price, license, and offer their software—and how this aligns with your needs.

Hardware and Storage

The hardware and storage requirements of a DAM deployment depend largely on the scale, capacity, and reliability requirements of the envisioned system, as well as the vendor's overall software architecture.

In cloud or full-scale SaaS models (that is, the vendor provides the hardware off-site), your hardware costs could be almost nonexistent. The cloud/SaaS model works well for many marketing organizations, where capital budgets may be small or nonexistent. Large enterprises with global marketing groups also tend to prefer the SaaS approach.

Scale—from a hardware perspective—influences both the capacity requirements as well as the geographic distribution of the system.

If you have users in Los Angeles and New York, for example, and both work on the same large files, some vendors might require that you have installations in both locations; clearly, this will affect your hardware costs.

Capacity dictates the following:

- The amount of processing power (servers) required to support the number of users, volume, and kind of media processing they require. For instance, if you expect to work with a significant amount of video, your hardware (processing) requirements will be significantly different than if you were working with many images, graphics, or design documents.

- The amount and kind of storage required. Video—especially HD video—can consume hundreds of gigabytes to terabytes of storage.

In theory, proper management of heavyweight media assets can reduce enterprise storage—not an insignificant expense—as duplicate copies across multiple shared drives are rationalized. However, in practice, greater and better management services will also expand the number and types of assets in your enterprise. While this will surely bring more value, it will also consume all that extra storage capacity you were hoping to save.

Reliability dictates the number of additional servers you need to fulfill defined or assumed uptime, redundancy, and quality-of-service (QOS) requirements, as well as devices for regular repository backups.

Individual vendors' DAM software architectures can have a significant impact on hardware costs. Over the past decade, enterprise vendors have moved toward more efficient and scalable *n*-tier architectures, based primarily on application servers. Depending on their implementation, they may be horizontally scalable, meaning that you can add processing power to the tier that needs it. The most common architectures have five tiers: client(s), Web server tier, application server tier, media processing engines, and database tier. Other architectures may compress their tiers. For instance, the media processing engines may sit on the same tier as the application server or DAM application, as shown in Figure 2.1. As Web technology has rapidly advanced and HTML5-based interfaces have been adopted, the internal desktop client has increasingly been replaced by Web clients.

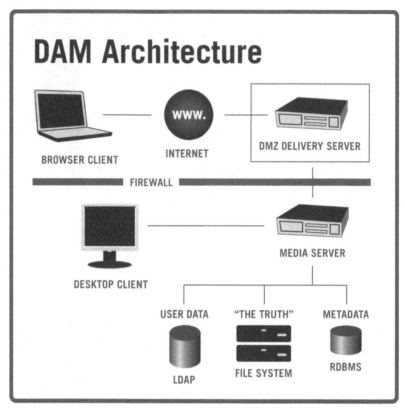

FIGURE 2.1
A DAM architecture example.

As should be evident by now, understanding the vendor's software architecture can dictate your hardware requirements and influence cost. You may need multiple individual servers to improve scalability, capacity, throughput, or reliability. Be sure to include this in your deployment, especially if you plan to phase your growth over time.

Most DAM deployments require client-side hardware, such as PCs or Macs, particularly for creatives using desktop design, layout, or video-editing applications. Even cloud/SaaS deployments need this hardware because users will need to work on assets in their local environments before checking them in or out. Will you need new desktop machines? You may, but you'll need to test your existing environment before deciding whether to upgrade.

Software-as-a-service models are an interesting alternative, particularly for marketing organizations. The vendor provides the hardware—often a full data center—as part of the service. In some cases, the vendor will also provide service-level guarantees. Vendors amortize the SaaS hardware costs across all users of the hardware and factor them into the monthly per-user fees. For marketing organizations, these purely operational costs fit nicely into monthly budgets, just like website hosting fees, PR, or analyst services.

Cloud/SaaS installations may charge fees for additional disk storage beyond the base amount, usually per terabyte of storage. They may use a similar metric for bandwidth costs.

The SaaS approach doesn't fit as well in enterprises that aim to draw down a capital budget and keep ongoing operational expenses to a minimum.

On-Premise Networking Versus Cloud-Based Provisioning

While we could have placed networking within the hardware discussion, we break it out separately to highlight specific cost considerations that come into play when working with large volumes of digital media files or very large digital media files.

Networking in on-premise environments for DAM systems has been a hidden and rarely discussed cost area. If, however, you are moving large numbers of files or very large files around a broad geographic region, networking becomes crucial. Consider once again the case in which users in Los Angeles and New York both generate and work with 300MB print-ready PDF files or video digital dailies. Moving those files back and forth for review and approval with regional printers or postproduction people could be cost prohibitive using traditional networking hardware.

Public cloud providers such as Amazon, Google, and Microsoft handle cloud-based networking. With built-in scalability and redundancy, and "anywhere" access via an Internet browser, most are now pre-enabled for mobile and tablet access. The cloud-based systems in a SaaS environment are more future-proofed for newer devices reaching the market, such as smart watches and the Internet of Things (IoT), where sensors are used to connect everyday items like refrigerators and lighting systems. The cloud becomes the digital nervous system that enables all things to be connected.

With the advent of the cloud in the enterprise at various levels, we see a sea of change in IT's place and role in the businesses of the future. Cloud-based operations are leveling the field between the capabilities of larger corporations and those of even small start-ups. This constantly shifting landscape is changing not only in applications but also in "bring your own devices" (BYOD), security, and governance. The cloud is blurring the traditional lines of what constitutes the term *enterprise* and how agile organizations can be—and at what cost.

One of the potential downsides of moving processing and software applications to the cloud is taking a hit on bandwidth, none more so than when processing large files, particularly video. Even using a BYOD approach, IT and finance departments need to work together to understand the implications of these strategic moves and plan mitigating strategies, for bandwidth load and the human fatigue (people get bored and less productive) associated with waiting for an application to behave correctly.

In scenarios that need to use and share high-resolution assets and video, File Transfer Protocol (FTP) isn't fast enough, and it strains bandwidth. A number of DAM vendors, and particularly those focused on broadcast media management, employ User Datagram Protocol (UDP) file acceleration software to increase load and download speeds. UPD sends chunks of data from one place to another, using the most effective methodologies available. You'll usually pay for this indirectly, since these tools are OEMed by DAM vendors (meaning they use software developed by someone else and pass the cost on to you).

Within the DAM industry, Signiant and Aspera have become the most common engines to transmit large files across the networks. They each claim a 100–200-fold increase in speed over HTTP and FTP protocols on a standard Internet transmission connection. A DAM strategy as it relates to the use and reuse of high-resolution assets can have a significant effect on bandwidth load—and company morale. Some vendors approach this as an add-on option, whereas others use metadata and version control. If assets could be tracked through their entire workflows and lifecycles, the actual need for high-resolution assets could be factored out until the final edit was needed to publish the content.

Metadata and Taxonomy Development

Technically a subset of consulting and customization, metadata and taxonomy development is another critical part of digital and marketing asset management that vendors only generally discuss. However, as it can be one of the primary hurdles to successful deployments and can affect DAM adoption, we believe it deserves mention. The cost of metadata and taxonomy development and management varies greatly, based on the level of granularity required to categorize or tag assets to meet your asset management and distribution goals.

As discussed earlier, you need to have metadata to be able to retrieve media assets. A taxonomy is a specific, defined classification scheme for information and the relationships among pieces of information. Thus, metadata (information about the asset) must be applied to the asset at some point prior to, during, or just after its entry into the DAM repository. Further, the system must make it searchable and accessible to appropriate people. To make the assets retrievable, you need to ask several questions:

- What information should be captured and made available for search and retrieval?

- What will be the standard or common conventions, lexicons, vocabularies, taxonomies, information tags, and formats?

- Who needs to access it?

- What do they need to access?

- How do they want to access assets and by what search criteria or navigational path?

- Who will be responsible for entering, maintaining, and, possibly, policing metadata in the system (performing librarian, "cybrarian," or "metatorial," services)?

Your team will need to put some initial thought and work into the information model that surrounds your media assets.

Traditionally, there have been three ways of meeting this need:

- **Buying a taxonomy off the shelf:** This option is very common in the STM (scientific, technical, medical—including pharmaceutical) community. Usually, these preexisting vocabularies also require modification and extension, which means you still need to resort to the following two options.

- **Hiring or assigning in-house resources to create and maintain the vocabularies:** It's always a good idea to foster internal expertise in this area because your own staff will know your subject domain the best. Internal resources, however, often have the time and expertise only to maintain a metadata model rather than create one from scratch, so you may need to turn to the following option.

- **Contracting with an external consultant or firm:** You may need to contract outside sources to work with you to create the model and train you or your subject-matter experts in maintaining it.

This last service can be provided by the vendor or, a better choice, by independent third-party consultants who specialize in taxonomy development and metadata models. Your enterprise may already have certain taxonomy standards in place for other content technologies, such as WCM or enterprise search. You may be able to leverage those standards and reduce your development costs and time.

Overall cost depends primarily on how simple or complex a metadata model you need, as well as the scale of your system. Your team's ability to develop a model, gather the required information from expected adopters and constituents, and assemble it into an effective metadata model will also affect your costs. Be sure to budget for this area because it is essential to the use, deployment, and success of your system.

CAVEAT

Metadata models and taxonomies continually evolve and thus have hidden recurring costs. You may need several tries to get it right, or several iterations and evolutions over time to make it fit the real usage and asset access patterns of your users. Don't expect your model to be perfect and set in stone from day one. It will change and evolve. Be prepared to have a process in place to change the model as your team's understanding of the system grows and your users' needs, access patterns, and preferences evolve. Budget for someone to be responsible for this area—with the power to make any changes to it.

Consulting, Configuration and Customization

DAM software alone does not a system make. Put another way: "It's the process, stupid!" Critical to all usage and success is how well the system fits into or supports the creative, production, and distribution workflows of your organization. To that end, you will likely need training or consulting to configure or customize (respectively) the system to fit the specific needs of your enterprise. DAM software installations usually take a few days. For SaaS deployments, it can be mere hours. Implementing and optimizing the system, however, can take months or even years to complete if it's a global, high-volume implementation.

As with other enterprise software deployments, try to think of a DAM deployment as a process and not a project, especially because you can expect configuration, customization, integration, migration, and training costs to exceed the software costs by 2–8 times. Consulting and customization costs typically depend on size and complexity of the deployment and can run anywhere from 0.5 to 5.0 times the cost of the software.

Historically, DAM technology has largely been a mix of off-the-shelf software and custom-developed software. This has two implications. First, it means buyer beware; the demo you see during the sales process may include more than just the standard features. Be sure to ask whether everything you see is, in fact, part of the out-of-the-box (or OOTB) software product. Second, it means that many vendors anticipate some level of customization in every deployment. Be sure that you understand whether you will need these services and if your chosen product requires customization.

In recent years, most vendors have moved toward more configurable software products. With this software, you can make changes to the DAM system, user interfaces, visibility (or hiding) of features, media processing capabilities, metadata and security models, and (in some cases), automation of workflows, without having to call the vendor or an integrator and pay per-hour fees. Configuration typically requires user training or minimal consulting services for one of your team members to become knowledgeable and proficient. These products may reduce your implementation costs by providing configuration interfaces, rather than requiring customization, which entails additional programming.

During the early assessment phases, ask many questions about which product features and capabilities can be configured and which require customization. If possible, get reasonable ballpark statements of work prior to signing the contract. Whenever possible, test the product with your own assets before proceeding. (Doing this will also give you a chance to see what the "bulk ingest" is like or how the batch-import functionality performs.)

Integration with Other Systems

In the early days of DAM, the systems generally were an island, operating independently of any other systems in the enterprise. Today, however, DAM is rarely a silo. Often, a DAM is taking in metadata from a Product Information Management system (PIM) or a Product Lifecycle Management system (PLM), or ingesting completed assets from Adobe Creative Cloud or a Creative Operations Management (COM) platform. If you're working in an organization with physical archives, you may have a Collections Management system or a home-grown data management system, which would manage metadata that would be vital to facilitate asset findability.

On the distribution side, DAMs are often pushing assets to a web content management system (WCM), a marketing automation tool that's managing campaigns, or to a printer (not just for marketing collateral, but also for packaging production or point of sale material for a tangible product company). Yes, a printer—print is far from dead!

Today, the costs for integration might exceed what you spend for DAM licensing alone, especially in a complex environment. For more on this topic, see Chapter 11, "Mixology: DAM in the Digital Marketing Cocktail."

Related Applications and Services

Digital and marketing asset management systems vary in the services they provide. For example, most systems provide basic search facilities or media processing services, such as extraction, transformation, or transcoding. If these services don't fit your needs, you may need alternative search or media processing engines that can cost tens of thousands of dollars. Similarly, all DAM systems provide security features and security models. However, additional capabilities such as single sign-on (SSO) or integration with LDAP or Active Directory for authentication are available only as add-ons. Be sure to budget adequately for the full solution you defined and envisioned for your enterprise.

Support

Support is an ongoing cost for as long as you have your DAM system, and it usually includes the cost of system upgrades and patches. Three different levels of support tend to be available: 5 days per week during "regular" business hours, 24x5, or 24x7. Note that for the first flavor, those hours are usually based on the business hours of your vendor, not necessarily *your* normal business hours. Some vendors also offer an additional "platinum" or "premium" support, which means you have a dedicated support resource or requests are prioritized for an additional fee.

If you adopt a SaaS system, support will be included in your monthly fee. If you have an on-premise installation, your support costs will generally be 15%–25% of your initial licensing fee. All the more reason to negotiate well up-front—because your ongoing total cost of ownership will be lower, as well.

Training

I've had several clients who have said "training is dead," "no one wants to be trained," or "this has to be as easy as my iPhone apps or no one will use it!" This is foolish and short-sighted thinking. A DAM system is far more complicated and feature-rich than your typical iPhone application. That's not to say it shouldn't be user-friendly and intuitive, but much like driving a car, all potential users not only need an education-oriented overview of what a DAM is for and how it supports the strategic intent of your business, but also need a detailed functional overview, so they are clear on what the system can do for them. It's important to communicate to system users the "what's in it for me" at this stage, in order to facilitate adoption.

You'll want to be sure to budget for this as an initial, up-front expense, and also plan to record the initial training sessions. The most successful organizations I've worked with all have very personal and detail-oriented training programs, and don't even let users use the system until they've gone through training. Don't even bother to buy DAM software if you haven't planned for and budgeted for this crucial phase.

Ongoing Operations

Ongoing operations costs include administration or librarian costs, software maintenance costs, networking charges, training and support costs, and occasionally storage costs. In a SaaS model, most of these costs (with the exception of training and librarian costs) will be included in the monthly fee. Self-administration helps to reduce support costs and increase autonomy. Some vendors encourage training an internal guru to provide the first level of support and problem triage.

There is no such thing as a free digital and marketing asset management system.

Adjustment Costs

Introducing DAM into an enterprise can be disruptive. This disruption provides an opportunity to change or restructure business processes—particularly to introduce new automation and structure around digital media—and to offer new services to a variety of constituents inside and outside the enterprise. While change is good, it is neither free nor easy.

Enterprises frequently overlook or misunderstand the true cost of organizational change. These "adjustment costs," which refer to the costs of organizational change that accompanies the introduction and deployment of new technologies, are inevitable. We have not seen any fixed approach for fully estimating and allocating these shared costs across all of the affected areas across the organization. With the evolution of DAM from largely departmental installations to a more centralized managed "IT infrastructure" layer, new personnel and organizational issues will emerge.

Content Costs

With DAM systems, you deal with content across any possible form of media: video, text, image, film, etc. You may have costs for any licensed or rights-managed content that you plan to manage with your DAM system. From a process perspective, you incur costs in selecting which content to elevate to an asset and in extracting and converting assets and metadata from legacy, homegrown, or prior vendor systems into appropriate formats for the DAM system. Every system has a process for ingesting, tagging, and extracting metadata, yet not all metadata entry can be automated. You may have content preparation, validation, and librarian costs. Further, some DAM products do not perform content preparation, fulfillment, and delivery processes very well, so you may have to pay additional manual labor costs.

A Final Note on Metadata

Determining whose responsibility it is to ascribe metadata can become a thorny and persistent problem for DAM implementations. We encourage you to ask your vendor or integrator for case studies and best practices for metadata management, and to use conferences to network with peers about how to manage the "people" part of metadata. This is as important, if not more important, than the DAM technology you select.

The DAM Maturity Model

If you need to justify an investment in DAM, one way to do so is to demonstrate how a lack of effectiveness in DAM may be hindering you or your organization. For this task, we recommend the DAM Maturity Model.

In 2012, Real Story Group, in partnership with the DAM Foundation and other industry leaders, created an open source model whereby companies could measure their DAM effectiveness. In 2016, Real Story Group used the Model to create a Web-based application called RealScore, allowing our subscribers to not only measure their effectiveness, but also benchmark themselves against their peers.

Using the model, you can measure your DAM maturity based on 15 dimensions across the following four categories (see Table 3.1):

- **People:** The human roles, responsibilities, and interrelationships in an organization's use and management of DAM

- **Information:** The material and related descriptors that enable the use of an asset

- **Systems:** The related components that work together to facilitate the lifecycle of assets

- **Processes:** The repeatable set of procedures and operations designed to realize each stage of an asset's lifecycle

When it comes to building a business case, it's important to note that a large number of IT and software projects regularly fail to deliver in one way or another, including the following reasons:

- Cost and time overruns

- Major bugs

- Unhappy users

- A final result that looks nothing close to the initial scope

Projects continue to fail, despite the fact that IT technologies and processes are more mature now than they were only a few years ago. Furthermore, if traditional IT projects are excluded from the sample and only those related to content management and digital asset management are considered, the success rate would be even lower.

So how can you improve the odds for success in your DAM projects? While having the right set of tools and technologies is important, these factors alone are insufficient to ensure success. An organization must consider and address varied challenges across human-, information-, and systems-related aspects. To do that, you need to follow a structured and repeatable methodology.

Effective implementation of a DAM project includes not only addressing technology-related aspects but also tackling those that relate to governance, people, and processes. As with other large enterprise content management (ECM) projects, a DAM implementation requires careful planning and development of a holistic strategy to address all categories of challenge. To begin any such initiative, however, an organization needs to know

- Where it currently stands. Or in simplified terms, the organization needs to be aware of its current state. This is also known as an "as-is" state, or the current state of the organization with respect to technology, processes, people, and organization.

- Where it wants to be (also known as a "to-be" state or the final state the organization aspires to reach). Based on an organization's business objectives and vision, it decides where it wants to be in the short term as well as the long term.

- How to do a gap analysis based on the as-is and to-be states. The organization then must determine what steps to take to progress from one state to another.

In short, an organization needs an approach that allows it to do all these things in a structured way. The DAM Maturity Model can be downloaded at http://dammaturitymodel.org/.

TABLE 3.1 THE 15 DIMENSIONS OF THE DAM MATURITY MODEL

People	Information	Systems	Processes
The human roles, responsibilities, and interrelationships in an organization's use and management of DAM	The material and related descriptors that enable the use of an asset	The related components that work together to facilitate the lifecycle of assets	The repeatable set of procedures and operations designed to realize each stage of an asset's lifecycle
Technical Expertise	Assets	Prevalence	Workflow
Business Expertise	Metadata	Security	Governance
Alignment	Reuse	Usability	Integration
	Findability	Infrastructure	
	Use Cases		

People

The first category in the DAM Maturity Model is composed of the dimensions described in the following sections (see Table 3.2).

The People dimensions represent the human roles, responsibilities, and interrelationships in an organization's use and management of DAM. Oftentimes, organizations believe that buying a technology will solve the majority of DAM challenges they face, however, having the right people and the right skills in place is equally important.

Technical Expertise

The organization needs to have key technical capabilities either in-house or via an external partner. Models such as the ITIL v3 (https://en.wikipedia.org/wiki/ITIL) and ISO/IEC 20000 (https://en.wikipedia.org/wiki/ISO/IEC_20000) offer a helpful guide for defining technical roles and responsibilities.

TABLE 3.2 PEOPLE

Dimension	Ad Hoc	Incipient
Technical Expertise	Exposure to the application of DAM technologies, including managing repositories and workflow systems.	Casual understanding of DAM technologies, often starting in the form of content management systems and centralized document repositories.
Business Expertise	Exposure to the use of DAM technologies, including repositories and workflow systems.	Casual understanding of the value of DAM, often starting in the form of using content management systems and centralized document repositories.
Alignment	Exposure to the use of DAM terminology, including ingestion, cataloging, transformation, transcoding, distribution, and so on.	Casual understanding of the need for DAM, often starting with using and creating content management systems and centralized document repositories.

Business Expertise

Business expertise refers to the employees' and management's understanding of fundamental DAM concepts in support of the organization's core mission. To promote an organization's DAM practice, the organization should use clearly related and defined roles as a starting point. Examples include the following roles:

- Asset owners
- DAM managers
- Rights managers
- Reporting analysts
- Product managers/ channel managers

- Metadata managers/ librarians
- Archivists
- Asset creators
- Sales/marketing managers

Formative	Operational	Optimal
Demonstrated experience with implementation of named DAM systems and core competencies, such as ingestion, cataloging, transformation, transcoding, distribution, and so on.	Managing repositories and workflow systems is core to IT with organized knowledge transfer.	Understanding and participating in forecasting enterprise DAM needs in preparation of future business requirements.
Demonstrated experience with implementation of named DAM systems and core competencies, such as ingestion, cataloging, transformation, transcoding, distribution, and so on.	Assets managed through repositories and workflow systems; a core function with organized knowledge transfer.	Understanding enterprise DAM capabilities to uncover current and future asset value.
Demonstrated collaboration to extract value from named DAM systems with core competencies.	Active collaboration using cross-functional teams to manage the improvement of asset repositories and workflow systems with organized knowledge transfer.	Proactive use and refinement of DAM capabilities to uncover current and future asset value.

Alignment

Alignment is the collaboration between technical and business areas using the value of DAM to achieve the organization's mission (see Table 3.2). This collaboration provides the capability for groups to anticipate the needs of one another with complementary strategies.

TABLE 3.3 INFORMATION

Dimension	Ad Hoc	Incipient
Assets	Disorganized, with no policy or organizational strategy.	Common repositories and policies.
Metadata	No metadata (file name only); disorganized; no policy or organizational strategy.	Inconsistent asset tagging; department-level common repositories and policies.
Reuse	No reuse.	Inconsistent, unplanned, or unsupported reuse.
Findability	Employees spend excessive time searching for material without finding it—often resorting to the re-creation of assets.	Search engine(s) adopted and indexing started.
Use Cases	Unstructured meeting of organizational needs; no value applied to user scenarios.	Project-level requirements gathered, but with no end-to-end context.

Formative	Operational	Optimal
Centralized organization and policy.	All new repositories and asset types registered with defined standards and practices for authoritative asset management.	Assets prepared and authorized for use and reuse across multiple channels, with organizational understanding of authoring for different intentions.
Conforming vocabularies for organizational use.	Enterprise taxonomies created; all new repositories and asset types registered and related.	Defined standards; defined job responsibilities; enterprise taxonomy in use; metadata is complete and travels with asset; metadata changes are tracked; ongoing refinement.
Development of a reuse strategy and planned reuse of specific assets.	Execution of a reuse strategy across all assets.	Discovery of new uses of assets beyond original intention.
Indexing completed; usage patterns reviewed, leveraging vocabulary terms for further refinement.	Implementation of specific enterprise and/ or federated search mechanism.	Search and classification becomes a central service with business-driven variants seamlessly delivering relevant assets and metadata by role; search mechanisms continuously improved.
Program-level requirements gathered; beginning to apply end- to-end context.	Well structured, organized, and prioritized; all users identified with known input and output expectations; dependencies, prerequisites and interrelationships identified.	Framework in place to define, measure, and manage existing and new use cases; systems validate.

Information

The second category in the DAM Maturity Model is composed of the dimensions described in the following sections (refer back to Table 3.3).

The "Information" dimensions allow you to measure the material and related descriptors that enable the use of an asset. As stated in Chapter 1, "What Is Digital and Marketing Asset Management Technology?," an asset isn't an asset without its corresponding metadata—otherwise, it's just a file. These dimensions allow you to assess and plan how well you're preparing for—or managing—the information around your assets.

Assets

Assets (with regard to information) refer to managing the hierarchy of authoritative digital assets—their creation, classification, usage, and distribution. It defines the following key lifecycle stages and how metadata is handled at each stage:

- **Ingestion:** How an asset is created or imported into the DAM system

- **Versioning:** The management of different iterations of an asset

- **Derivatives**: Works in progress during the creation of new assets or subassets

- **Media Processing and Transformation:** The capability to convert an asset from one format to another and create different renditions by way of transcoding and transformation

- **Distribution:** The delivery of a final asset

Metadata

Metadata is specific information describing the nature or "about-ness" (categorization) of assets. This information provides methods to support categorization and classification by defining taxonomy models and vocabularies, including ontologies, folksonomies, and schemas.

Reuse

Reuse refers to an organization's repurposing of assets across multiple channels and an organization's appreciation of single asset authoring for different intentions.

Findability

Findability is the way that users navigate services to search for and retrieve assets. In DAM, search mechanisms work hand-in-hand with the organization's services and information models.

Use Cases

Use cases—from simple to very complex—describe the functional capabilities of DAM systems. Every organization's needs are different, and these differing requirements and use cases are defined as *scenarios*. Scenarios also include generic capabilities such as personalization, collaboration, and multichannel delivery. Use cases are a method for planning an implementation that will clearly address end-user and organizational needs.

Systems

The third category in the DAM Maturity Model is composed of the dimensions described in the following sections (see Table 3.4).

The "systems" dimensions represent the related components that work together to facilitate the lifecycle of assets. While DAM systems might operate independently of other systems, that's increasingly rare. Usually, assets are dependent on data that originates in other systems, or must be integrated with distribution systems downstream.

Prevalence

Prevalence defines how broadly the DAM efforts are permeated throughout the organization.

Security

Security is the extent to which the actual asset access reflects enterprise entitlements—including capabilities for single sign-on authorization, authentication, policy enforcement, users, roles, internal/external access controls, rights management, and authenticity.

Usability

Usability refers to the ease of use of various user and configuration interfaces.

TABLE 3.4 SYSTEMS

Dimension	Ad Hoc	Incipient
Prevalence	Individual.	Scattered siloed efforts.
Security	No asset-specific security regime in place.	Specific security.
Usability	Usability is disjointed with no cohesion or commonality; employee frustration rates are high.	Single platform with use of raw (out-of-the-box) tools.
Infrastructure	Planning is reactive between business and IT.	Project-specific implementations as directed.

Formative	Operational	Optimal
Initial attempts to combine or adopt DAM across the enterprise by executive champions.	Successful enterprise initiatives completed and in use.	Enterprise integration aligned with company culture prior to implementation; DAM has become commonplace.
Defined, centralized security controls and system standardization.	Security controls clearly defined and enforced throughout the organization at an asset level.	Security is an organization-level, shared service with processes to address new threats in a timely manner; automated.
Some multiplatform support; creation of user- or persona-specific tool interfaces.	Remote multiplatform enabled; user-centered design with formal user-feedback collection.	Driven by dynamic business needs; effort meets expectations; multilingual; multiplatform; consistent UI; intuitive; instructional; integration with SAP or other business intelligence system.
Proactive but informal business and IT coordination beyond project specificity.	Joint change management or governance leading to proactive implementations.	Formal coordination and mutual accountability with agreed timelines, roles, and goals.

Infrastructure

Infrastructure is a set of interconnected systems and organizational elements that provide a framework to support the entire structure of enterprise DAM.

Processes

The final category in the DAM Maturity Model is composed of the dimensions described in the following sections (see Table 3.5).

The "process" dimensions represent a repeatable set of procedures and operations designed to realize each stage of an asset's lifecycle. As mentioned previously, technology alone won't solve your DAM challenges: process capabilities, in addition to having skilled people in place, will contribute equally to your success.

TABLE 3.5 PROCESSES

Dimension	Ad Hoc	Incipient
Workflow	Few or no standardized procedures for asset lifecycle.	Basic process analysis leads to some informal workflows.
Governance	Employees self-govern.	Scattered policies and few formal procedures.
Integration	No intentional integration.	Brute-force integration between systems and processes.

Workflow

DAM systems apply and in some cases automate business processes to manage digital assets. These processes are composed of workflows to maximize resources and minimize latency, which in turn increases asset availability.

Governance

Governance ensures that the DAM strategy and policies are properly implemented and the required processes are correctly followed.

Integration

Integration facilitates efficient data transference within and between systems and processes.

Formative	Operational	Optimal
Formal workflows with limited automation.	Automated processes span systems and departments; command and control of standards.	Continual refinement and managed experimentation; workflows are standard practice; measurable performance indicators established.
Centralized development of structure and codification of procedures; management support.	Policies and procedures widely disseminated and enforced; ownership and responsibility in place; communication and training on policies throughout organization.	Active refinement; utilization of end-user feedback; an established means to measure and motivate.
Integration vision is complete, including people, process and technology, and understanding of common paradigms.	Integration vision is in practice, using well-defined, documented paradigms.	Real-time and seamless integration enables common user experience.

CHAPTER 4

DAM Technology Services: Asset Creation and Management

V endors usually call asset creation *ingestion*. The meaning of "creation" in the DAM world differs from its meaning in other content technologies, such as with a web content management (WCM) system. In those technologies, content creation actually happens *in* the system: A user logs in, types in content, and then publishes it to a website. The DAM system "creates" an asset when it ingests a file and accounts for its corresponding metadata. Both the file itself, such as an image or video, and its metadata may have actually been *created* outside the system, but in the context of the DAM system, the *asset* is not *created* until it and its metadata are *ingested*. As such, unlike WCM or DM systems, DAM systems typically don't offer native creation services. You're expected to *author* files in some other tool. That's why "connectors" to native applications such as Avid Interplay, Adobe Premier, Adobe InDesign, and so on, are so important.

In a DAM system, ingestion typically combines several smaller and more discrete services, capabilities, and user actions to turn files into assets in a single large step. In this context, we discuss ingestion in some detail, as it is one set of capabilities needed in the overall asset creation process.

Ingestion

Ingestion is one of the core capabilities in DAM software. It's how files, media, and metadata are transferred to the system, prepared for system admission, and become managed assets. Prior to ingestion, you often set up what are called "hot folders": an easily accessible, topic-based grouping for assets of particular types or categories.

Ingestion includes the set of capabilities or services that determine the following:

- What types of files are supported (see Table 4.1)?

- How are files uploaded, copied, or moved from their current location into the DAM, or referenced at their current location from the DAM system? (By "reference," we mean a digital "pointer" to the content's actual location, which can be on essentially any kind of storage—see "Copying Versus Moving Files.")

- What asset processing can be performed at this initial stage?

- How are the files and metadata "turned into" assets?

TABLE 4.1 TYPICALLY SUPPORTED FILE FORMATS AND CODECS

Supported File Formats	.3gp, .aac, .flv, .m4v, .mov, .ogg, .vc1, .3g2, .amr, .gfx, .m4a, .mpa, .mfx, .wmv, .avi, .asf, .h263, .mp3, .mpg, .rm, .wma, .ac3, .dv, .h264, .mp4, .mpeg, .ts, .vob
Supported Audio Codecs	AAC, AMR-NB, DV Audio, MPEG-1 (mp1, 2, 3), Windows Media, Audio, Pro, AC-3, AMR-WB, orbis, PCM (16-, 24-, 32-bit), Real Audio
Supported Video Codecs	Cinepack, DV Video, DVC Pro 25, DVCPro 50, DVCPro 100/HD, Flash Video, H.263, H.264, HuffYUV, M-JPEG, MPEG-1, MPEG-2 (PS and ES), MPEG-4/XVID, Microsoft MPEG-4, ON2 (VP5, 6), Sorenson, Theora, VC-1, VC3/DNxHD, Windows Media Video (7, 8, 9), XVID

Supported File Types

Your first task is to consider what types of files the DAM system supports. Because digital asset management and marketing asset management have emerged out of multiple technology and industry origins, such as publishing, broadcasting, and content management, a digital asset management system may have a bias regarding the types of files it supports. Many can handle almost any file type. Others handle only video, images, or a smaller range of rich media file types. For example, some may or may not handle Flash files.

By "handle," we mean the product is able to recognize or process the file type, even if not completely. In its basic sense, processing means that the system recognizes the file format, can create a thumbnail and other "renditions" of the file for preview or proxy use, and, in some cases, can transform or transcode the file into other file formats. Some systems can create the standard and basic thumbnail for the file but cannot perform any transformation functions.

Processing can be the ability to extract or pull out of the file embedded information, in various formats, such as IPTC, EXIF, XMP, file attributes, Microsoft Office file metadata, key frames, and closed-caption text from a video. Regardless, the DAM system must support the specific set or breadth of file types with which your users will be working. For instance, if you're using a specific Camera RAW file format or video format, make sure that the system can support it and its manipulation into other required or low-resolution formats.

DAM vendors—especially those with systems that can generally handle all file types—try to ensure that adding new file types is well planned for, and their approach to this may be an important discussion to "future-proof" your system.

Copying Versus Moving Files

DAM systems either transport files from their initial location, such as on the users' desktops, to the common, often centralized repository, or leave them where they are and create a reference or link to them in the repository. This architectural distinction is important.

The first case implies several things. First, it implies that you have a mechanism for transferring the files. Enterprises typically transfer or upload files using either FTP or HTTP. Which protocol you use should depend not on what the system provides, but on what your requirements are. For example, FTP works well for small- to medium-sized files and for bulk file transfer, but it may not be reliable enough for very large files. You don't want a file transfer to fail halfway through a large file, and then you are unable to restart it from the point of failure. Alternatively, you may need to transfer files through a corporate firewall, and the IT department may not leave open the FTP port for security reasons, so you have to transfer the files using HTTP over port 80 or, in some systems, FTP over HTTP on port 80. The key point is that the IT department may dictate the File Transfer Protocol, which will affect the speed and reliability of delivery. Therefore, be aware of the File Transfer Protocols supported by the DAM as part of ingestion.

Most DAM systems copy the file into the repository, duplicating its storage. They establish the file in the repository as the "master," creating a centralized repository, and leave the original file where it was. This feature ensures that if the transfer fails, you still have the original file and can attempt to upload it again.

Alternatively, the DAM system moves the file, rather than just copying it, and then it removes the file from the original location when it completes the transfer. As a service, this variation is atypical, but some systems support it. If the system supports moving the file and the ingestion fails, it should leave the file where it was. Based on your particular needs, you need to examine where you want to store your files. You may want to leave your huge video files on a production server in Los Angeles rather than in the main repository in New York.

This example leads into the second case: references or "pointers" to remote files. Many asset management systems, particularly smaller workgroup and original desktop systems, ingest a file by creating a thumbnail of it and leaving it where it originally sat on the file system. Without going too far into storage management territory here, in this case, the management system treats *the file system as a virtual repository* and simply catalogs what is on the file system (which could be distributed across numerous machines). Simple consumer DAMs and media management systems, such as iTunes, function in this way.

For an enterprise, this approach works best for very large files, such as HD video or print-ready PDFs. In this case, you don't want to incur the transfer cost but need to be able to catalog and rendition the assets in place and reference them and their storage location from the DAM system. This approach also comes in handy if you later move to a secondary or tertiary storage and archive format.

The downside: If the storage location becomes inaccessible or the file is moved, the asset becomes inaccessible. Systems often try to recover or catch this circumstance and provide a mechanism for recovery, but the resolution may require significant human intervention.

Bulk Upload

DAM systems typically can bulk upload, do batch transfers, select, and transfer multiple files to the DAM in one fell swoop. The systems vary in how they support bulk upload, specifically, in how they handle the failure and recovery of the upload. For example, if you're ingesting 1,000 files, what happens if a file fails to transfer due to a disk, network, or file system error? Are you able to restart the transfer from the point of failure? Does the system ignore the one file and continue, telling you at some point that it failed? In the worst case, if one file fails, the whole batch fails. Similarly, what happens when the system fails in processing a file? Perhaps the file format is corrupted or the system doesn't recognize it, so it can't extract the metadata or generate renditions. Does the system make a list of all the failed files? Is this list visible to the person uploading the file, to the admin, or both?

ALERT

Failed file recovery during ingestion is a critical part of the asset creation or ingestion workflow. If the system doesn't handle it well, you will take a productivity hit—possibly a substantial one.

Compound File Handling

Compound files contain, embed, or reference other assets. Examples can include Adobe InDesign or Illustrator documents, books, catalogs, brochures, ZIP archives, PowerPoint presentations, or a DVD. Generally, compound assets are master container files that embed or reference other files, which may or may not also be compound.

Uploading compound assets introduces a number of challenges for a DAM system. How they're handled varies from product to product. The first challenge is how the system marshals the externally referenced and internally embedded files. In other words, how much work do you have to do to upload a compound file? Quark and Adobe layout documents commonly reference files that live elsewhere on the file system. Are you required to gather all of these files into a location and upload them as a batch? Do you need to create a special ZIP file that contains the full document so that the system has and can reference all the linked files? Or does the system provide mechanisms or tools to perform this process for you?

PowerPoint files are a common example. A slide deck may reference images and files that live elsewhere on the file system. They aren't assets (yet), but they need to be included in the upload. If the system doesn't handle this process properly, when you try to download the file from the system, it will have unresolved links to files and may corrupt your presentation. Compound files become what we generally call "compound assets." We discuss them in more detail in the section "Asset Creation" later in this chapter.

Video Ingestion

Unique to video and media-specific workflows, the video ingestion process can vary due to the complexity of video. Ingestion can include transferring digital video files, converting from analog videotape or formats to a digital format, or receiving a streamed or live video feed, particularly in archiving and producing video. Even in deep video use cases, however, we're increasingly seeing fully digital (or "file-based") workflows.

If you work with digital video, you need to consider the system's transcoding capacity. How many video files can the system convert at one time to other typically lightweight formats for preview and distribution? In some use cases, the system may need to bulk ingest tens or hundreds of longer video clips, which will later be segmented into smaller clips. With the increased use of high-definition video as a source format, more users need to transcode HD to low-resolution formats, particularly for distribution to the Internet or mobile devices. An increasing number of systems can transcode to Windows Media and QuickTime formats, with some variation in the file resolution, bit rate, and encoding. HD files require significant storage and processing to convert, particularly for longer videos of more than half an hour. Often, the system uses dedicated hardware and software to create "transcoding farms," resources that increase the capacity and throughput of the process.

Metadata is yet another concern. What, if anything, does the system extract from the video in order to later retrieve it? Because of the video asset's rich visual and audio content, video ingestion and automated video metadata extraction are more complicated and involved. Video ingestion typically includes the following automated processing:

- Extraction of file information, as would occur with any file

- Extraction of key frames and their associated time codes

- Extraction of closed-caption text, if it exists, and indexing that text back to the time code and frame in which it occurs

- Extraction of final production script information with time codes

- Optional conversion of speech into text, specifically into a text transcript that indexes the text back to the particular frame in which the spoken words occur, thereby enabling full-text search to locate sections of relevant video

- Optional identification of the speaker or, in some cases, speakers

- Transcoding the full video into desired stored renditions

When you are considering production video ingestion, the volume of simultaneous streams or feeds can be another initial capacity concern. Does the system have the ability to receive and handle the volume and speed of the feeds? Can it then transcode the received video into other specific formats in a timely manner? Can it recognize camera location or geospatial data? Beyond that, video ingestion includes the manual (human) or automated tagging of the video from the feed with metadata, either in real time or with some delay.

Video ingestion workflows vary significantly. Depending on the system, these ingestion processes can require significant individual attention for specific features, for handling file formats, bit rates, and compression, or for addressing specific workflows. Because of video's complex and demanding needs, a subset of DAM vendors have chosen to focus specifically and solely on video or media asset management. You may need both an image-centric and a broadcast media-centric system; ask lots of questions about how they work together.

Metadata Extraction

As mentioned earlier, ingestion includes processing the incoming file. Typically, it includes extracting or pulling out the embedded information or data that becomes metadata in the DAM system. The information could be embedded in the file as file attributes in various standard formats, including IPTC, EXIF, and XMP; as Microsoft Office file implicit metadata, such as author, date, and modified by; or as (in the case of video) scene changes, key frames, time codes, closed-caption text, or possibly through speech-to-text conversion that indexes text back to the video.

Systems vary widely in the kinds of file attribute and metadata extraction services they provide. You need to be sure that if your workflows or metadata include information stored in standard formats, you can extract and store—or map and store—in the system. More generally, you need to understand which information the file system can extract for a given file type and which it cannot.

External Metadata

Our discussion thus far implies that the system stores the metadata in the actual media file itself. In many use cases, the metadata persists in a separate database or in a separate file, such as an Excel spreadsheet, that is married with the file at ingestion. In some cases, this metadata file may itself become an asset later in the process (in which case it's sometimes called a metadata *sidecar*). Not all systems support marrying separate metadata to individual assets. If this feature is important for your use case, ascertain whether the system provides the capability.

Additionally, metadata can live in an external system and be pulled by the system at ingestion. We expect this ability to access or query external systems for metadata to become increasingly standard. It can assist many workflows where the information already exists in other systems and simply needs to be aggregated in one place. The file is part of the asset, providing increased value and searchability to both the file and to the asset.

Automated Ingest

Note that new videos are not created in a DAM system, but existing content is brought into (or ingested into) the system from a variety of sources. The video feed can be from a live source or from a previously existing one. Live sources can be via a video camera, a satellite, or even a smartphone. Existing content may be ingested from tapes on videotape recorders (VTRs) or may already be in digital form on another server.

The ingest module in a DAM system allows simultaneous recording from multiple sources of feeds. There is typically functionality to schedule recordings at predetermined times and dates, and they can be set for one time or repeating. There is also a tool to monitor ongoing recordings and check the details of past recordings. Monitoring tools let users preview the feed while it is being recorded instead of waiting for the recording to finish; this feature permits them to make notes of interesting parts of the video and subsequently use them.

FIFO Ingest

Some DAM systems record feeds from live sources (for example, satellite) in a temporary storage area. The amount of this storage is configurable based on requirements. Frequently, the First In, First Out (FIFO) rule is followed here; that is, recordings continue until the temporary storage is full, and then the system continues to record by erasing the first-in (oldest) video content.

This temporary storage feature is useful in recording feeds even while operators are not monitoring the feeds. Unless it's deleted or overwritten, the video is available in the temporary storage. Users can browse the contents of the temporary storage and extract clips by marking in and marking out relevant portions of the video segment.

There is a plethora of details about ingestion technology. A DAM package that does this well is able to do the following:

- Ingest a wide array of formats.

- Ingest in multiple ways, such as uploading via web browser, FTP, mobile, and tablet devices. Most vendors are adopting simple drag-and-drop interfaces for ingestion.

- Read any previously embedded metadata at ingest. Some vendors require this to be configured at setup, whereas others do this out of the box with minimal to no configuration.

Asset Lifecycle Services

Asset lifecycle is the set of services for creating, reading, viewing, updating, versioning, and deleting assets and metadata. It also includes locking of assets, such as check-in/check-out, and governing of "asset uniqueness."

The system must provide asset lifecycle services. Without them, not much would happen. You need to determine what functions the system provides as part of these services:

- How does the system detect unique files and handle duplicate files?

- How does the system handle the versioning of assets and metadata?

- How does the system handle asset deletion, as opposed to asset removal?

- Does the system support a simple locking or version control mechanism, such as check-in/check-out?

- Does the system support asset or metadata placeholders, so you can store a job or create a collection before it contains assets?

- How does that placeholder support work?

- When and how does the system back up assets?

- How does the system restore these assets in the event of system failure?

- How does the system archive assets?

Asset lifecycle services tend to operate in the background, particularly if you work with the system through the DAM or from within a third-party application. If you plan or need to develop custom extensions to handle particular workflows or scenarios, access to these services via APIs or Web Services may be particularly useful.

Detecting and Determining File Uniqueness, Duplicate Handling

As discussed previously, ingestion focuses on the creation of new assets in the system. As such, the ingestion services need to work with asset lifecycle services. In particular, upon receipt of a submitted file, the system must be able to detect and determine whether the file is a duplicate of a file in the repository. If so, the system must determine what to do with the file and any associated metadata. For unique files, the system creates a unique identifier for the asset, which it keeps throughout the lifecycle.

The detection and determination are a bit of magic. Most DAM systems determine whether the file is unique by performing an algorithmic calculation that examines the file at a binary level and determines whether the mathematical result on the pattern of bits duplicates one it already has. The system typically performs a checksum calculation or calculates a hash (which you can think of as a kind of digital fingerprint), providing a value to compare with those already stored for files in the system. Many systems use the well-known MD5 hash algorithm. In theory, it is possible for two different files to give rise to the same checksum, but in practice, this is not something you need to worry about with MD5 (it's only a concern with lesser algorithms). Still, you do need to know what happens when and if the system discovers a duplicate file, and you need to know in advance what you want it to do for your situation. Does the DAM system

- Ignore the asset?

- Ignore the metadata?

- Give notification that it is nonunique or is a duplicate?

- Version the asset?

- Create a new, duplicate asset with a different identification?

- Append the metadata?

- Overwrite the metadata?

- Version the metadata?

All of these are potential outcomes for handling duplicate files. Systems vary in their duplicate handling capabilities. You need to understand your workflows and how you use assets in order to align them with the various systems' duplicate detection and determination process.

Asset Creation

Asset creation is another fundamental asset lifecycle service. It usually occurs after the system determines a file to be unique. Asset creation gives an asset a unique identifier. It may also invoke other services, such as allocating space for the file and the metadata; extracting, storing, and indexing the metadata; transforming to create predefined stored renditions; and performing any other initialization processing.

Some systems may provide flexibility on aspects of asset creation. For example, some systems allow asset or metadata "placeholders." In instances in which the system only retrieves the metadata, this function creates a placeholder asset, which only has metadata, but there is no file associated with it; the file is added later. The reverse is also possible; the system creates the asset, but the metadata, or the bulk of it, can be married later.

With this flexibility comes increased power—and increased complexity. The system can handle a wider variety of workflows, such as allowing delayed or separate addition of assets and metadata. On the other hand, users must learn how to identify which asset(s) to marry with which metadata properly. They must also be aware that metadata may exist without files and files may exist without meaningful or searchable metadata.

Versioning

Upon duplicate detection, the system may create a new version of the asset. This implies that the system can maintain a lineage of historical snapshots of the asset and the metadata as they change. The asset's identity doesn't change; rather the system uses some mechanism to identify it and associate it with its various versions. Asset versioning facilitates creative workflows, tracking, and managing work in progress (WIP) among users. It also facilitates distribution workflows, in which different versions are distributed to people over time, or where one version is released while creatives work on the next version. Finally, it also facilitates historical views of the asset and its metadata over time, which has its own value (see Figure 4.1).

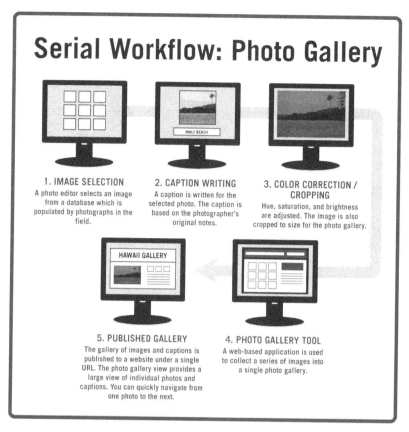

Serial Workflow: Photo Gallery

1. IMAGE SELECTION
A photo editor selects an image from a database which is populated by photographs in the field.

2. CAPTION WRITING
A caption is written for the selected photo. The caption is based on the photographer's original notes.

3. COLOR CORRECTION / CROPPING
Hue, saturation, and brightness are adjusted. The image is also cropped to size for the photo gallery.

5. PUBLISHED GALLERY
The gallery of images and captions is published to a website under a single URL. The photo gallery view provides a large view of individual photos and captions. You can quickly navigate from one photo to the next.

4. PHOTO GALLERY TOOL
A web-based application is used to collect a series of images into a single photo gallery.

FIGURE 4.1

Creating a photo gallery is a common DAM scenario that requires versioning and multiple contributors. In a Serial Workflow scenario, versioning allows for rollback to a previous version or saving multiple resolutions of an image for publication to non-Web channels, such as print.

As with other content management technologies, versioning services vary from vendor to vendor. Some systems version the asset and its metadata as a unit. Some systems version just the asset; the existing metadata carries forward but can be changed. Other systems allow independent versioning of the asset and the metadata. A major version number indicates a change to the asset itself, such as a color correction to a photo; a minor version indicates a change to some metadata, such as changing the caption on the photo.

Systems also vary on version access. Some systems may present and provide access only to the latest version; others present and allow access to the entire history and any individual version. In both cases, security services typically govern access to a version. Lastly, systems vary on whether they allow purge or removal of obsolete versions. Many systems don't allow deletion of versions because it can introduce additional integrity problems.

As with all features, you need to be clear on your needs for versioning. Specifically, what do your users need in their creative and distribution workflows and business processes?

Asset Removal and Deletion

The asset lifecycle also handles removal or deletion of assets. Most systems distinguish between removal and deletion/purging. Removal usually implies that the system removes the asset from most users' view but retains it for administrator access. Deletion or purging means that the system has completely eliminated the asset and its metadata. Some systems have two-phase approaches. First, you mark an asset for deletion, which quarantines it. Then a privileged user—usually the administrator—deletes it.

Security services govern all users' ability to remove and delete assets. Storage management services may reclaim and compress the now-unoccupied space. The distinction between removal and deletion and the two-phase approach provide less risk of accidental deletion and greater control over who can do what.

Version Control Via Simple Locking

Most asset management systems support a simple exclusive-lock mechanism called *check-in/check-out* or CI/CO. It allows you to check out an asset, which "locks" and gives you exclusive access to it and its metadata. Neither the system nor other users can change the asset while you have it checked out. Other users, however, can view and download the asset while it is checked out.

Version control is a useful feature for some creative workflows to guard against unwanted changes.

Of note, if you download a compound asset for editing, this function also locks the assets contained in the compound asset. If someone downloads an asset that's part of a larger compound asset, you need to decide if that locks the compound asset as well.

CI/CO should not be confused with traditional database "concurrency" mechanisms that govern transactions. Every asset management system has concurrency mechanisms because some part of the system exists on a database, such as metadata storage, but it is usually buried deep in the system and not exposed to users.

DAM packages that manage asset lifecycles well have the following capabilities:

- They handle the creation, reading, viewing, updating, versioning, and deleting of assets and metadata.

- Multiple rights, roles, and permissions can be assigned at the asset level.

- The analysis of use, reuse, and shareability can be captured.

- An archive of the assets is present and available at the end of an asset's lifecycle.

Media Processing

Media processing differentiates asset management systems from other content management technologies. Media processing takes multiple forms in a DAM system. It handles the changing, transforming, transcoding, extracting from, or inserting into the rich media file of the asset. It also deals with the automation of these processes, the integration of third-party tools to perform these functions, and the types of files these functions can support or process.

Proxy Creation

One of the critical functions of an asset management system is providing lightweight viewable renditions of the asset in an easily accessed format. This typically means creating and storing multiple individual renditions of the same asset at ingestion—for each version of that asset. This includes a representational thumbnail of the file content to identify and associate with the actual asset, as well as one or more other appropriate "proxies," which are renditions that allow users to experience the asset easily and quickly, without accessing the often significantly larger master asset.

Transformation, Transcoding, and Rendering

Transformation, transcoding, and rendering are primary media processing capabilities that change assets from one form to another. Transformation refers to the processing of images, while transcoding refers to the processing of video, audio, or other time-based assets. These functions exist primarily to create a thumbnail, preview, proxy, or other renditions of the file, but they also produce on-demand output forms of a file for distribution or use. These three processes include several capabilities; they can do the following:

- Take an asset's file and turn it into different formats, sizes, scales, file types, and resolutions.

- Create a new audio or video file with different characteristics, including format, resolution, encoding, bit rate, or frames per second. For example, they can create the low-resolution videos that can play in a variety of devices or in Microsoft's Windows Media and Apple's QuickTime formats over the Web.

- Create animations, such as animated GIFs, consisting of a series of renditions of pages from a document, brochure, or catalog; slides from a PowerPoint deck; or frames from a video, to a give quick visual flavor of its content.

- Separate layers in a multilayered photo or layout file for deeper representation of the asset. Conversely, they can combine layers into an output format.

- Segment a PowerPoint file into its individual slides, each as an asset, or further separate individual slides into their constituent parts, each potentially as an asset. Conversely, they can generate on-the-fly slides from assets or presentations in PDF, Flash, or PowerPoint formats from collections of individually selected slides.

- Generate appropriate output formats for mobile or handheld devices.

- Extract audio/text.

- Extract storyboards from video (see Figure 4.2).

- Extract content and instructions from digital signage control systems.

FIGURE 4.2

An extracted video storyboard from Oracle, which offers several lightweight DAM capabilities.

Metadata Extraction and Insertion

Media processing also includes all of the system's metadata extraction and insertion capabilities. They include the ability to pull different and variously formatted metadata out of files and, in certain distribution scenarios, insert metadata into the file so that it stays with the file outside the system.

Third-Party Media Processing Tools

Asset management systems vary in their implementation of media processing. Do they make it available or configurable to users? What kind of media processing do they support? How adaptable is the system to adding support for processing continually emerging new media formats?

Most systems integrate third-party tools or engines to perform the work. They include but are not limited to

- Graphics conversion and metadata extraction tools.

- Video encoding.

- Transcoding and indexing tools.

- PowerPoint slide manipulation tools.

- XMP engines.

Some systems are more limited or flexible. You need to drill down into this area to ascertain that the system can do what you need it to do and that your users have easy access to those functions. As mentioned previously, it's important to be sure that your DAM vendor has architecturally "anticipated" the ever-growing assortment of file types and provides a clear upgrade path for new utilities and file tools.

DAM packages that handle media processing well have the following capabilities:

- Modern-day file formats can be read and processed.

- A multitude of transcoding can take place.

- Metadata will travel with the digital assets and won't be lost during the process.

Taxonomy Management

Finding information in your company is likely chaotic. A taxonomy is a great start to planning how assets should be classified and who should have access to each asset. A taxonomy should encompass the major touchpoints within your organization that represent how people need to find things. It likely encompasses the company organizational chart, with the roles of the individuals within the organization, including partners, clients, and stakeholders. It should factor in logical navigation by users and enable people to access information and content in common sense, logical ways. Like most things, change is constant, and taxonomies must adapt to change.

There are a number of differing approaches to managing taxonomy within DAM systems. Some products offer only a rigid way to tweak or change a taxonomy; others give administrators more flexible tools to change, import, and tweak. Some vendors seek to move the taxonomy away from the hierarchical navigation by using controlled vocabularies, collections, and relationships through the clever use of metadata. Other products allow for several different taxonomy structures depending on the business silo for which they are applied.

Metadata, Controlled Vocabulary, and Schema Support

Media companies strive to maximize the commercial potential of their assets and improve the quality of their programming. They want to repurpose, reuse, and enhance their content licensing revenues. Key to all of this is capturing the metadata associated with the assets. Enriching video assets by adding relevant metadata through the asset lifecycle increases the chance that relevant videos will be retrieved as required—without spending unnecessary time trying to locate the video assets from the library. We'll examine different aspects of metadata management in greater detail in the following sections.

Metadata is data about data. Without it, your assets are essentially unmanaged. Metadata drives the security of these assets by way of rights, roles, and permissions. It drives the taxonomy, navigation, and the hierarchical structures of your data. Most of all, it drives findability, personalized experiences, and business intelligence.

Findability

If you or your users cannot find digital assets or aren't aware of them, your DAM initiative will fail on multiple levels. The ability to find and reuse assets is a critical component of any DAM strategy. Vendors approach the area of search and findability in a variety of ways. Carefully review vendors against your search and find use cases and criteria. We explore this extensively in Chapter 5, "DAM Technology Services: Search, Retrieval, and Navigation."

Establishing the Initial Information Model

Vendors typically provide a minimum set of services to assist your team in establishing the initial structure and organization of the asset management system's information model. Most provide, or partner to provide, more—at a cost. Depending on the scope, breadth, and complexity of your deployment, this could entail significant consultation expense. However, it is well worth the effort to get the core of the information model right the first time. Regardless of how it's created, the system needs to support the model you need. Aligning your needs with the information model is a critical step. Be aware that, whatever information model you establish as your initial model, it will change—and sometimes sooner than you expect it to.

More important than support of the initial model is understanding the underlying features of the system that support the development and maintenance of the information model, and their ability to support changes to the model.

The organization of assets and metadata is fundamental to both an asset management system and your application of the system within your enterprise. Successful asset management implementation requires organizing the metadata and the assets to fit the business processes and workflows of your enterprise, matching both *the way your users currently work* and the way your DAM team determines *how the processes need to work.*

Metadata management includes

- The definition and management of assets and metadata.

- The structure of predefined or evolving metadata—such as keywords, controlled vocabularies, or taxonomies—that can be defined, managed, and applied to assets.

- How assets are cataloged, tagged, ranked, rated, or annotated.

- How assets can be organized into groups, folders, or collections, or related to other assets, as in compound assets and configurations, and what can be done with and within these groups.

- The degree of flexibility administrators have in adapting or redefining the structure of the metadata model or schema.

Metadata Definition and Organization

A DAM system fundamentally must provide metadata definition and organization capabilities. DAM products vary in how flexible or limited these features are. A system can allow users to define a great deal of information:

- What information can be captured as metadata for each asset.

- The definition of metadata types or sets.

- The definition of metadata items.

- The grouping or clustering of metadata items into metadata types.

- The data type of the metadata item value.

- Whether structured data types are supported, such as an address consisting of street, city, state, and postal code.

- Whether the metadata item values are predefined, restricted to a controlled vocabulary, or free-form, user-provided text. If they are controlled, whether only one or multiple values can be selected.

- Whether a metadata item is required or optional.

- The default metadata item value(s).

- Whether the metadata item value is user provided or automatically extracted by the system. If so, how it is mapped between the extracted field or value and a specific metadata item.

- What implicit or explicit relationships exist between assets, including contains/is contained in, uses/is used by, derives from, parent/child of, sibling of, unidirectional/bidirectional, and how these relationships are implemented.

- What implicit or explicit relationships exist between metadata types and between metadata items, both on the same asset and on different assets, such as inherited metadata, multivalued fields, nested metadata, cascading metadata, conditional values, and rules.

- Whether multiple metadata types or sets can be applied to a single asset.

- Control of the visibility of metadata types, items, or values.

- How users can group or categorize assets and whether assets inherit metadata values from the group.

- The point in time at which the metadata is captured—synchronous with asset creation, ingestion, or delayed/later.

- If an asset is required or not (for example, you can have a metadata "record" without an asset).

- How and where the metadata is stored. Specifically, is it a literal database schema (that is, database tables are metadata records) or an abstract model implemented on top of a database, proprietary file system, or search engine?

- Whether they understand multiple taxonomies and polyhierarchy.

- Whether and how they can connect to an external enterprise reference repository.

In short, many possible subfeatures enable metadata definition. Because there's so much variety in the structural support of metadata among products, you must know what metadata you need to capture and then deeply probe into what and how a product supports it. Systems may be limited in what they provide for metadata or asset relationship definition. This may limit your information model and restrict what you can capture and represent. For example, most systems may allow only one set of metadata per asset. This limitation can be problematic because, over time, the metadata that's useful to some audiences may change or different use may require different metadata.

If you know how the system implements control over the visibility of an asset's metadata (or whether it allows multiple sets of metadata to be applied to the asset), you can determine whether the system works for you. Otherwise, you may have to work around the system to capture the metadata you need over the lifetime of the asset.

In addition, how the system implements or stores metadata may lead to trade-offs. For example, a system that uses database tables as the metadata structure may provide great flexibility in the initial definition, but it may cost significantly more in terms of future modification and maintenance. It could require system downtime to change or evolve the metadata schema and migrate existing values to the new structure. A system that uses a more abstract model may provide easier maintenance and dynamic changes to the metadata schema—without downtime.

Dynamic Schema

Some systems can dynamically create the metadata schema and define new metadata types. You don't need to stop or quit the system to add to or modify the schema. A system that supports dynamic schema creation can build the metadata model interactively—in front of your eyes—or read it from metadata definitions embedded in a file. This function can provide flexibility, adaptability, and power for maintenance and for working with files from other systems, partners, or organizations.

If the system supports both dynamic schema and XMP metadata extraction, you can leverage XMP to provide metadata about an asset, which the system could then use to create new assets dynamically. You can read more about XMP in the section "A Special Note About Standards" in Chapter 7, "DAM Technology Services: Architecture and Administration."

Community Tagging

There are different kinds of metadata. Increasingly, asset management systems incorporate contemporary Web concepts of community and the collective view of the crowd to enhance collaboration and ease of use. One example of these concepts would be informal, bottom-up, evolutionary approaches that dynamically weigh keywords based on popularity, rather than the more traditional, formal top-down, predeveloped taxonomies. Other forms include community tagging (folksonomies), asset ranking, user-defined tags and categories, and comments or annotations.

Grouping Assets

All asset management systems provide mechanisms for grouping assets, and those groups are based on various types of metadata. Typically, the system supports named, hierarchical groups, folders, or collections, much like folders on the file system. (Note: We use the terms *folder* and *collection* interchangeably here.)

Some systems place an asset in one or more named folders or collections. In this instance, the system places a reference to the asset, rather than a copy of the asset. The system doesn't duplicate the asset. Typically, the security system governs the privilege of creating new folders; for some users the hierarchy appears to be fixed, while it can be tailored for others.

Some systems allow collections to be dynamic, basing the content of a collection on an attached query or "saved search" performed at the moment the collection is opened. As a result, the collection content may vary from instance to instance, reflecting changes to the result set, and from user to user, illustrating the effect of access controls and potential visibility permissions on assets. These folder and collection facilities are useful for general organization and for restricting visibility or enhancing collaboration.

Permissions on folders can restrict visibility to assets. Some systems allow users to share folders privately with other users. This ad hoc collaboration and sharing of assets works well for project-centric workflows. Combining permissions and sharing may allow one user to put assets into a folder while others may only view them. This function suits DAM distribution applications in which approved marketing assets can be distributed for use in the field by putting them into a known location. If an asset can be placed in one or more folders, some systems can determine all of the locations in which that asset can be found. This capability is very useful for assessing an asset's visibility and accessibility. You will need this feature in some form, so be sure to examine and inquire how the system provides, implements, and presents it through the user interface (UI).

For broadcast media scenarios, a media-centric asset management system needs to support collections or groups of different types of assets. For example, the still images, promotions, trailers, and the program video could be one collection. Another collection could be a TV series and different episodes within the series. A slightly different requirement is the ability to attach a document to a video asset, such as the script of the program, the rights information, or some other related document. The use cases may differ, but the DAM system's ability to support asset collections makes it more intuitive for all users.

Implicit and Explicit Metadata

Metadata is added to the asset while it is being ingested and any time after that. We can think of two types of metadata in the DAM world: implicit (sometimes also called technical metadata) and explicit or descriptive metadata.

Implicit or technical metadata (as the name suggests) refers to the technical characteristics of the asset itself (such as format, size, and storage location). Implicit metadata does not require a human to define it because the system captures or creates this technical metadata automatically and adds it to the asset during the ingest process itself.

Descriptive or explicit metadata refers to the details or "about-ness" of the video clip and any other information that is deemed useful about the content of the video. This information is explicit because usually human beings are required to define it. Some of this information is manually entered by users at different times using a data entry form. The different fields and metadata vocabularies available in this form are usually decided at implementation time and configured accordingly. Consider what sorts of explicit, descriptive metadata will help your users find assets more easily and incorporate such information into your retrieval plan.

Controlled Vocabularies and Thesauri

To enforce discipline when categorizing content (for example, assigning tags to an asset), systems can enforce a controlled vocabulary by allowing users to choose from a preset list of categories or tags. The admin users have permissions to add or edit the controlled lists while others just make use of them to ensure consistent asset classification throughout the organization.

Certain vendors support the thesaurus functionality. Here, they make use of the "relatedness" concept to improve the relevance of search results. By creating a hierarchy of categories (such as country-state-city), you can broaden or narrow the searches. Figure 4.3 shows an example.

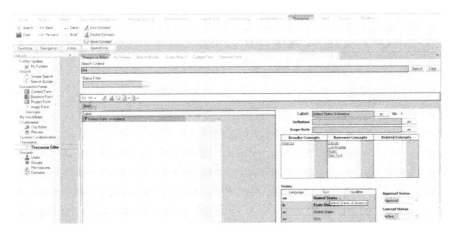

FIGURE 4.3

The Imagine Communications Thesaurus Editor allows you to enter broader, narrower, and related concept tags associated with a given term.

Automated Metadata Extraction

Certain rich media assets may already have other useful descriptors available like subtitles or captions. Some systems permit subtitle imports into the database and use them to create the index for search. Similarly, speech accompanying the videos can be converted into text using speech-to-text plug-ins and then can be used for search. Of course, the utility of that functionality is determined not so much by your asset management system, but by the efficacy of the plug-in provider.

Another important issue to note is the extent of the support for multilingual metadata. Users should be able to enter metadata in different languages and search accordingly.

As content increasingly is ingested from mobile journalists, the geospatial data associated with it is also captured as an important piece of metadata. This is particularly the case for video analysis in military applications and increasingly for law-enforcement or sports-oriented tracking scenarios.

Asset Relationships

While the preceding metadata aspects pertain mainly at the individual asset level, we should also consider the asset collections and associations between assets.

An asset is usually available in different formats, resolutions, and even versions; only one instance is generally considered to be the gold copy. The system maintains the relationships between the different asset avatars (renditions) and uses the relevant asset based on context and purpose. For instance, when a user is browsing search results, a low-resolution version of the asset is displayed. However, when the same asset is delivered to the editors for finishing touches, the high-resolution version of the same asset is available. Similarly, if an asset is being published to the Web, the appropriate format of the asset is distributed.

Another take on this is the genealogy of assets; here, we reference the parent-child relationships of a video and subclip, or derivative clips from the parent video. The system should keep track of such genealogy for many purposes, including rights management.

Enterprises often want to establish relationships among assets. These can reflect real, physical relationships, or establish a relationship that enhances the inner representation of the information from an information-management perspective.

Systems vary significantly, both in the kinds of relationships that they can support and how they implement and present these relationships to users. Some systems provide higher-level structures that represent a prepackaged form of a specific relationship. For example, a "compound asset" acts as a container or parent to other contained or child assets. Other systems provide lower-level mechanisms in which you establish specific relationships and build higher-level structures. For example, a system may provide parent-child, sibling, unidirectional, or bidirectional links that you use to relate assets and build more intricate structures of related assets. A few systems provide both. As with all the other features, you need to understand your use cases, the information model you need, what the products offer, and how they implement their model.

Compound Assets

Compound assets result from the ingestion of compound files. As previously described, compound assets consist of or contain other assets. Generally, compound assets consist of master assets and contain or reference other files or assets, some—or all—of which may be compound.

Asset management systems vary in how they support, represent, handle, and implement compound assets. You will encounter many subtleties to compound assets in the course of examining your workflows around the creation, alteration, and presentation of compound assets. For example, systems vary in how they manage changes to compound assets. Some systems perform deeper decomposition of the ingested compound asset, such as taking apart an InDesign document or separating layers. The difference lies in what the asset management does with the embedded or referenced files in the document or with each individual layer:

- Does it make each an asset or keep them as some lesser, nonasset entity?

- Does it make them visible only within the context of the master, or can they be reached on their own?

- What does it establish for metadata for the embedded or referenced file? Or for the separated layer?

- Does it have its own metadata independent of the master? Does it have none? Or does it inherit most or all of it from the master?

- Does it establish a reference or link to the file as a placeholder if the file is not included in the upload?

- How does it handle changes to these files?

- What does it do with respect to the versioning of both the file itself and the containing master file?

With respect to PowerPoint files, the questions are similar: Does the system treat the file, each individual slide, or individual elements within the slides as assets?

You need to understand these subtle—but critical—distinctions because they fundamentally affect your information model, workflows, and experiences with the system.

Related Assets

In some cases, users want to create a bunch of "related or associated assets." For instance, when you select one asset, the system selects all of the other assets that are linked to it in some relationship, showing you that these assets are related and how to navigate through them. Examples include the following:

- A press kit that includes three data sheets, a company backgrounder, a FAQ, and the latest press releases.

- A package of assets for display on a specific Web property, such as three different encodings of a video clip, two different still images representing the video clip, and two different approved captions for the clip.

- Related images of an item for a given model number, such as an image of a faucet that (depending on the finish of the faucet) corresponds to different SKUs in a catalog. Each has different metadata in the DAM, yet they all correspond to the same model of the faucet.

Asset management systems can provide one or more prepackaged structures, end-user features, or lower-level definitional mechanisms that establish links or relationships among assets. Common mechanisms include parent-child links, sibling relationship, unidirectional, bidirectional, one-to-many, many-to-one, many-to-many relationships, or links. With these mechanisms, you can establish more complex relationships and structures of related assets. An administrator usually performs this task when defining the information model.

Configurations

In an asset management system, the term *configurations* describes the snapshot at a point in time of a bunch of related assets or related asset versions. Other content management systems might call these *editions,* or *products,* or simply *snapshots.*

Configurations come into play when you create an asset containing or relating to multiple existing assets and you want to capture the state of these relationships at significant points in time. For example, a brochure may include several photos, copy (text), graphics, and logos.

- What happens when you update an included photo and the photo asset is versioned? When you view the brochure, which photo version is presented?

- Can you see the former configuration as well as the latest, or only the latest?

- Can you go back to any point in history and see the configuration at that point in time? Can you, for example, see either the released configuration or the one you didn't choose?

- How does the system handle changes to related assets or compound assets?

- Does it even provide configurations or configuration management features?

- Can these configurations of assets be managed by the system? If so, how?

- How does the system support configurations?

- Does it make them visible and easily understandable through the user interface?

Be sure to research this area diligently if it is important to your workflow. You may also want to share any "mission-critical" workflows with the vendor, such as an automated workflow with a postal office or printer.

Schema Change

The last area of organization concerns the degree of flexibility administrators have to adapt or redefine the structure of the metadata, such as the metadata schema or metadata taxonomy. Every asset management system allows you to define the initial scheme. That's great, but you have no assets at that point and no metadata. An absolute empirical rule of an asset management system is that the metadata organization or taxonomy will change, and you may need to change it much sooner than you expected.

Choosing a system that flexibly supports change will be critical to your success. Determine what kinds of metadata changes the system supports easily (that is, out of the box) without additional coding. Understand whether changes to metadata organization require you to bring down the system or can be done dynamically. Determine how the system migrates metadata from the old structure to the new, and find out if search indexes are affected by the changes.

It's a lot to digest. DAM packages that handle taxonomy management well have the following capabilities:

- Taxonomic structures are present and are used to group similar assets or projects.

- Users can navigate using taxonomic structures.

- Taxonomies are used to add parent categories on metadata entry (supports structured categories).

- Assets can be assigned to multiple taxonomies.

- Taxonomic structures form an integral part of the DAM architecture and are universal across search, data entry, and navigation.

CHAPTER 5

DAM Technology Services: Search, Retrieval, and Navigation

earch, retrieval, and navigation services dictate how users find assets, and search is one of the top reasons customers buy DAM software. Every application of asset management requires finding assets. Furthermore, nearly every workflow requires search at some point, because users must have a way to get to the assets they need. In asset management systems, search mechanisms work hand-in-hand with some of the organization services and information models outlined earlier.

As I've stated before, don't underestimate the importance of developing a user- and consumer-relevant taxonomy metadata structure before you purchase DAM software and migrate all your files into it. DAM systems do not magically make all your assets searchable without solid metadata planning and governance up front.

Structured Metadata Search

Despite the fact that you're working with rich media, DAM search mechanisms typically operate over the textual metadata. Most systems index all of the metadata; some may optimize for searching only certain fields or metadata items. The search index may be provided via the database, using SQL and the metadata stored in the database. It may also come through full-text indexing in the database or a built-in or added-on search engine, which either indexes the database or receives the metadata or files separately as part of media processing during asset creation.

Some more modern systems generate metadata based on image recognition, based on a training system that you provide. You'll pay accordingly for such sophisticated features.

Simple and Advanced Search

DAM systems traditionally provide two ways to search:

- A simple search in which search terms are matched against the full search index (versus looking for specific criteria in specific fields)

- An advanced search in which you can be more specific about your criteria

They both follow the paradigm of advanced searches in which you combine desired criteria. In the following sections, we'll break down the elements that play into successful searching within a DAM system.

Full-Text Search

For files containing text, the system might perform full-text indexing as part of the initial processing of the asset or as an additional service. The system accesses most rich media files through their metadata instead of indexing the visual or auditory content directly.

Rich Media Search

In addition, some vendors use third-party technologies that provide additional, non-textual search through image comparison or audio/phonetic recognition. These approaches continue to improve in accuracy, reliability, and performance, and they have become increasingly viable. Some systems use third-party speech-to-text tools to convert audio or video files into transcripts. In these cases, the system may search the transcript text and index it back to a time code in the audio or video file. The accuracy of the speech-to-text recognition has improved significantly but may still prove to be error prone. For accessing specific video or audio files, this is a powerful and advanced feature.

Most systems that handle video also provide mechanisms for extracting a sequence of key frames and presenting them as a storyboard for quick visual recognition and rapid access directly to a point within the video. Some enterprise DAM systems and most of the video-centric DAM systems can annotate video with text or other information for direct access back to specific points in the video, or via search to similar entry points in a long-form video.

Surfacing of Search Features

DAM products range widely in how the search features surface within the user interface. Systems that use text search engines may provide a richer search feature set. They may expose some of the engine's native search features like stemming, synonyms, thesauri, autocompletion, and recently issued queries. Some systems increasingly take advantage of built-in categorization support to help users find similar assets, providing clusters of categorized assets based on metadata. Several DAM packages can search on specific metadata fields. Their systems immediately download the results via a connector to the native application for editing.

Saved Searches

Depending on their roles, users look for certain feeds or types of content, so they search the repository for content that matches desired criteria on an ongoing basis (for example, looking for updated content from a particular source every day). To support this capability, DAM systems usually support periodic saved search queries. For example, the workspace consists of different folders that could represent different search queries.

Federated Search

The reality of media companies is that metadata exists in multiple data sources like enterprise portals, intranets, and other applications that are generally outside the DAM system. When you want to search against both the DAM and other enterprise repositories, support for federated search is needed.

Note that when it comes to the efficacy and relevance of search, DAM controls certain things, but for others, the onus is on you to ensure that you maximize search capabilities. Digital asset systems are responsible for the performance of search queries (dependent on multiple factors like numbers of assets, deployment configurations, and hardware capacities). Largely, you are responsible for the quality and accuracy of the metadata.

Since most DAM vendors have gravitated toward Lucene/Solr-based search software, the differentiation in the underlying software has been decreasing. However, what differentiates one vendor from the other using similar search techniques is the ability to render a UI and a UX around different types of users, offering the maximum amount of flexibility in terms of search criteria and how each application works to best service each user group. Although it all goes under the heading of search, it is the ability to find (using whatever level your roles, rights, and permissions allow the system to serve up) the very best and most contextually relevant information in good time and the best order.

Search is a complex beast; some vendors approach it using dynamic metadata working in harmony with dynamic workflows. Other vendors are much more static, which leads to more change management at the people level to make the system work.

Navigation

From a navigational perspective, systems increasingly use concepts like community tagging, saved searches, recently accessed assets, ranking, and recommendations to facilitate navigation to popular assets or to filter assets quickly. These concepts extend beyond the now standard hierarchical folder-based organization that people use to browse to assets or to jump to something they've previously located. Some systems may also provide hierarchical taxonomy or controlled vocabulary structures that are represented in the user interface by hierarchical folders. They may also use a search engine's categorization or faceted navigation facilities, presenting the categories in a similar or visually useful manner. Some systems allow you to scope your searches to a subset of the hierarchy. For example, you can look just in a folder or in that folder plus all of its subfolders.

Faceted Search

An area that's fast becoming standard in DAM systems is the concept of faceted search, similar to what is used on the public Web for e-commerce. Here, instead of a query builder in which you add criteria prior to searching, you start the search with a few basic criteria and then slice and dice the result set based on appropriate filters. While faceted search has advantages in terms of providing a better user experience and helping users refine searches, the experience is reliant on how fast the search engine responds to filtering results further. You may be familiar with faceted search from the Web; it's still relatively new to this field of technology.

In search and navigation, you must understand how your users look for and find information:

- Do they prefer to search?

- Do they navigate to their assets?

- How formal or informal is your taxonomical approach?

- How much information needs to be searched?

- How configurable is the display of the result set of the search engine? Is it a mass of Google-like pages where you still have to hunt? Or does it provide a more refined presentation of information and categories with which your users can really be productive?

- Which of the native features are surfaced in the UI?

- How well does the search experience scale with hundreds of thousands or millions of assets, or thousands of concurrent users?

You should consider some of the preceding questions when examining search capabilities. Figure 5.1 shows an example of this functionality.

FIGURE 5.1
Faceted search functionality in Vizrt Viz One.

DAM packages that offer robust search capabilities, simple or advanced, are able to meet the following criteria:

- They are able to use multiple metadata fields as filters; Boolean search is a higher level of functionality on top of this.

- They provide an application of search in a best practices user experience, perhaps using some interesting search options not seen elsewhere (such as search by CMYK or DPI).

- Full-text search is available.

- They are able to search for content in compound document types and PDFs.

- They offer full indexing of all (or close to all) documents, including multipage PDFs and a range of Office documents. Service is preferably out-of-the-box (OOTB).

- They use industry-standard metadata schemas, with the ability to add other metadata schemas that have shared and common vocabularies.

- They offer demonstrable experience working with third-party software that can enable rich media searching.

- They provide close integration with third-party software, *or* a basic tool is available for rich media searching.

- More than one type of rich media searching is available, *or* they offer excellence in one type of rich media searching.

- They offer autocomplete, stemming, or fuzzy search.

- They are able to perform searches in multiple repositories distinct from the DAM system itself, or they can be integrated with third-party software to achieve the same goal.

- They offer integration with third-party software to perform federated searches on a number of external repositories, or have a built-in tool that excels in performing federated searches in external repositories.

- The system has some ability to build queries to add criteria prior to searching and add filters postsearch to narrow results.

- Faceted search is well developed, and many criteria and filters can be applied.

- Faceted search can be fully customizable by the user.

- The search experience should be unaffected by scale (assets or user numbers).

- They are able to save searches or create collections/lightboxes.

- They are able to share collections and saved searches.

CHAPTER 6

DAM Technology Services: Asset Assembly and Delivery

So far, we've been discussing the creation, modification, and classification of digital assets: the production of content. Now let's look at the *distribution* of that content.

Asset assembly and delivery are primary uses of DAM systems. Enterprises often employ asset management systems in creative workflows and collaboration efforts as stores for designers' works in progress, as the conduit for managing the creative workflow, or as the final archive for their work—all from the creative or designer's point of view. Asset management, however, also involves the preparation for distribution of finished works to various channels or media. Whether it's a brochure that will be sent to the printer, an episodic video sent to iTunes or play-to-air, or the distribution of banner ads to websites, asset management systems can provide valuable capabilities to facilitate the effective preparation and delivery of digital media.

In general, assembly includes all those services that allow users to find, work with, and assemble assets into secure, finished works. Delivery includes all of the capabilities and integrations required to deliver assets to a system, device, location, or person. The capabilities outlined in the following sections could be used within both creative and distribution workflows. We have organized them in general sequence as part of the overall asset management lifecycle.

Collaboration and Storyboarding

Media and broadcast-centric DAM software contains tools that help users (such as television producers or journalists) put together stories from multiple videos. With a story script in hand, they can combine new and existing videos by searching for relevant videos in the archive, selecting specific portions from different videos, and adding them to a bin or a storyboard with a timeline. The work in progress is shared with producers, editors, and other teams, and they may iterate a few times before the final story is ready.

Note that they will be working with only low-resolution versions of these assets. The proxy versions generated are usually frame-accurate, which means that specific frames of the video can be annotated and marked. Once finalized, the edit decision lists (EDLs) are sent (electronically) to the editing team for finishing. Using nonlinear craft editors (like Avid Media Composer), they apply the edits to the high-resolution versions for on-air broadcast.

While the editing team uses nonlinear editing (NLE), media-oriented DAM products include editing software (usually referred to as rough cut editors) that provides simple video-editing functionality. These editors can play (or preview) videos with pause, rewind, and fast-forward controls, and they can mark in and mark out very specific portions of the video. It is not uncommon to find both web-browser-based editors (used for previewing remotely) and thick-client editors (usually Windows). In such cases, the functionality of the web-browser editor is often a subset of the thick-client editor's functionality (see Figure 6.1).

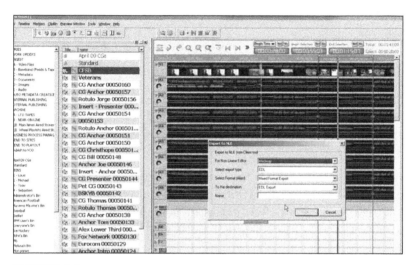

FIGURE 6.1
Exporting a selected portion of a video clip to an NLE from Dalet.

Another feature that is useful during storyboarding (and search) is the extraction of key frames of the video asset. Typically during video ingest, media-oriented DAM software extracts images of the video at specific time intervals, and these images serve as a visual table of contents for the video. For longer videos, this capability helps users easily zero-in on particular segments. These key frames can be generated not just based on time intervals but also with some logic pertaining to changes in the video shot (that is, how much one shot differs from previous shots). Depending on the configuration, users may have the ability to select key frames manually. Of the many key frames extracted, one is selected as the default thumbnail for the video (and is used when that video is displayed in the search results, for example).

The rough cut editor also can be used for adding audio effects like voice-overs.

In DAM software, marking up, annotating, and commenting on images and compound files are key features of collaboration. Most DAM software now includes this functionality, often via third-party creative operations management tools such as ConceptShare or globaledit. For even more effective collaboration, look for a tight linkage among the creation of collections, sharing, permissions, and workflow. Collections are essentially used to perform a wide range of DAM functions and are governed by extensive security controls.

Workflow

In this book, workflow means formal, structured processes around rich media assets that are enabled by the DAM. These processes can be automated or semiautomated. Semiautomated processes involve people, such as review and approval, in which reviewers take the asset, do a review, and submit the response back to the system. Fully automated processes involve system actors only.

Workflow facilities include the ability to define formal sequences of system-stewarded tasks within the asset management system. The system can perform these tasks automatically, or people can do them manually. The tasks have distinct states, transition and completion requirements, optional conditional logic, and optional time constraints.

Historically, these facilities have resided outside the asset management system or have been OEMed (meaning licensed from somewhere else, so it's not the original "equipment" of the company you're buying the software from). Depending on your use case, you may still want to have a separate, independent workflow or business process management (BPM) system that tells users what to do and integrates with the asset management system. See Figure 6.2 for an example.

The workflow facilities allow you to automate and schedule repetitive tasks. You can schedule and track multistep, multiperson, formal processes such as creating a brochure, selecting photographs, performing multistep legal review, and preparing assets for distribution to multiple channels. Workflow features can be very powerful and often require time to understand their capabilities, limitations, strengths, and weaknesses.

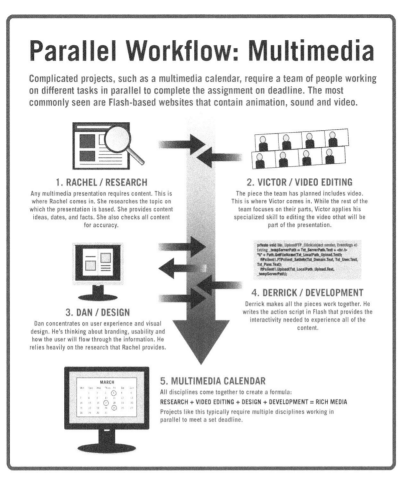

Parallel Workflow: Multimedia

Complicated projects, such as a multimedia calendar, require a team of people working on different tasks in parallel to complete the assignment on deadline. The most commonly seen are Flash-based websites that contain animation, sound and video.

1. RACHEL / RESEARCH

Any multimedia presentation requires content. This is where Rachel comes in. She researches the topic on which the presentation is based. She provides content ideas, dates, and facts. She also checks all content for accuracy.

2. VICTOR / VIDEO EDITING

The piece the team has planned includes video. This is where Victor comes in. While the rest of the team focuses on their parts, Victor applies his specialized skill to editing the video othat will be part of the presentation.

```
private void Btn_UploadFTP_Click(object sender, EventArgs e)
{string _tempServerPath = Txt_ServerPath.Text + <br />
"\\" + Path.GetFileName(Txt_LocalPath_Upload.Text);
ftPclient1.FTPclient_SetInfo(Txt_Domain.Text, Txt_User.Text,
Txt_Pass.Text);
ftPclient1.Upload(Txt_LocalPath_Upload.Text,
_tempServerPath);}
```

4. DERRICK / DEVELOPMENT

Derrick makes all the pieces work together. He writes the action script in Flash that provides the interactivity needed to experience all of the content.

3. DAN / DESIGN

Dan concentrates on user experience and visual design. He's thinking about branding, usability and how the user will flow through the information. He relies heavily on the research that Rachel provides.

5. MULTIMEDIA CALENDAR

All disciplines come together to create a formula:

RESEARCH + VIDEO EDITING + DESIGN + DEVELOPMENT = RICH MEDIA

Projects like this typically require multiple disciplines working in parallel to meet a set deadline.

FIGURE 6.2

Parallel workflows can't be managed by a DAM system alone; they require business process planning and, often, third-party tools.

Typical DAM workflow considerations include those shown in Table 6.1.

Before understanding the workflow engine's capabilities, you need to catalog your intended creative, ingestion, management, assembly, and delivery processes to determine which capabilities you need in a workflow system.

TABLE 6.1 DAM WORKFLOW CONSIDERATIONS

Workflow Feature	Comment
Serial and/or parallel workflows	Most systems support only serial flow.
Branching and reconciliation	Somewhat rare.
Predefined actions	Commonly available.
Automated system actions such as moving or copying assets to folders, removing or deleting assets, automatically uploading assets on a scheduled basis, or transforming assets as new renditions or for delivery	Varies.
Reusable workflow or process templates	Commonly available.
Specification and assignment of users, groups, and roles to tasks	Role support varies.
Notification of the state and status of workflows and workflow events	Commonly available.
Scheduling and tracking of workflows against the schedule	Varies.
Time constraints for completion	Commonly available.
Error and failure handling	Varies widely among vendors and products.
Scalability and robustness for large numbers of simultaneously executing workflows	Generally poor.
Security and observance of DAM feature and asset access controls	Usually built in.
Menu-driven or graphical user interfaces for workflow definition and status	Still rare but increasingly common.

Do not be unduly swayed by vendor presentations or even
vendor feature demonstrations when it comes to workflow.
Often these demos amalgamate features that you can't combine
without extensive consulting or custom development services.
Some vendors show you everything the system *could* do—and
count on your imagination to think it will work exactly like that
for you. Be sure to ask which features come out of the box and
which features require additional customization, configuration,
or consulting to address your workflow. Simple collaboration
features like annotation may be all you need.

Workflow is the management of technical and user tasks involved in
the media asset lifecycle, and it is one of the core technology services
provided by asset management software. Examples of technical tasks
include transferring a large media file from one location (server) to
another required server, generating a low-resolution proxy version
of the media asset during the ingest process, and converting the
media file into the required format prior to distribution. User tasks
refer to performing quality control checks on ingested media assets
or reviewing media files. Workflows usually involve a mix of both
technical and user tasks, and the workflow management module
orchestrates the different sequence of steps as the media asset moves
through different stages from ingest to archive.

One of the benefits of workflow services is that it can automate many
of the repetitive tasks shown in Table 6.1, so manual processing
errors are eliminated and users are available for other tasks. For
example, you can set a rule so that any media asset that has been
unused in the past week would be moved to a particular storage location. In this case, users would not be required to monitor asset use or
manually move assets to another location. Similarly, you can set up a
modified FIFO rule so that when storage is full, the least used assets
could be moved to another server.

Setting up these rules is important. The workflow module supports
the functionality for these rules; even more important is the initial
definition of these rules. While there are best practices and basic
principles, these vary, and the definition is based on an analysis of
the workflows and business processes relevant to your enterprise.
Vigilant workflow analysis forms a very important part of the DAM
implementation process.

Often, users are unaware of the different tasks the workflow engine is doing because they are done in the background in response to user-initiated or rules-based activities. Users can check the status of different tasks (or processes) and the completion status through workflow monitoring tools. Some asset management products support email notifications, although users typically tend to check status in workflow monitoring screens.

We've mentioned how workflow rules are defined during the implementation phase, but workflows can change over time and the asset management products often provide GUI-based workflow design tools. Previously, the vendor professional services team tried to understand your requirements and implemented corresponding workflows by writing software code (or in some cases, just configured the workflows for very common workflows). This meant that if you needed to change anything, you had to rely on the vendor team.

GUI-based workflow designers are intended to let you design custom workflows without the need to write code (see Figure 6.3). Customers use block-level diagrams and arrows to model their workflows, and behind the scenes, the software generates the necessary code. Graphically designing workflows helps to visualize the process and identify opportunities that lead to improvements.

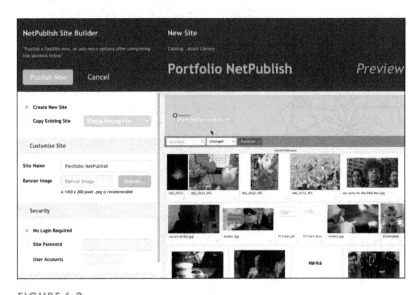

FIGURE 6.3

Workflow engine for producing FastSite/landing pages from collections by Extensis Portfolio NetPublish.

While workflow monitors are mostly used to view the status of running processes, some vendors analyze this monitoring data to help identify bottlenecks. For instance, you can check to see how much time was spent on different steps of the workflow and identify whether inadequate capacity is slowing down the entire process. This can lead you to identify the need to add another server to improve process speeds and decrease delays.

Likewise, you may gain insight that available server capacities are too high, based on utilization percentages, and decide to cut idling resources. This analysis need not be limited to devices or equipment but can encompass user tasks as well. If approval queues are very long, staff there may be overworked, or they may be waiting for assets to be available to them to start their work. Such resource-optimization techniques can help keep the broadcast content factory humming like a well-oiled machine—at least in theory.

Localization and Internationalization

As companies are increasingly global, it becomes more important to be able to allow asset managers around the world to search for and work with assets using an interface in their own language, and to be able to target multilingual messages. DAM vendors vary in their ability to do this. But what do localization and internationalization mean, exactly?

- **Localization:** The actual act of making a product appropriate for users in a given locale. While localization means more than translation, it still often implies some intense translation workflow requirements. It also means the actual localization of user-facing interfaces, including tool tips, contextual help, dialog and UI labels, error messages, and so forth.

- **Internationalization:** The capacity to localize. Theoretically, an internationalized interface can be localized. This typically means (among other things) that text strings (error messages, dialog labels, tool tips, and so on) have been segregated into separate resource bundles instead of being intermixed with code or binaries. It also typically means that the product is capable of rendering Unicode-encoded text.

Global organizations usually want to localize content. However, this process can be expensive and time consuming. Reusing the same assets in multiple geographies can save hundreds of thousands—or in some instances, millions—of dollars in hard and soft creation, production, and distribution costs.

Localization isn't just about the ability to have different versions of assets for different regions. Localization is critical to brand management. An enterprise must appropriately present its brand, message, and image in a given region. Localization is about using the right pictures and images, as well as sending the right message. For instance, colors have different meanings in different cultures: red in China connotes luck, whereas it means danger or anger in the United States.

Typically, local or regional offices handle these decisions. With the DAM system's localization functionality, you can provide consistent global access to enterprise assets 24×7 and support consistency of business processes and creative workflows regardless of region. You can both allow more regional autonomy and achieve global brand and message consistency objectives.

Localization Versus Internationalization

Localization sometimes blends with internationalization or multilingual support. Localization means much more than just translation, and multilingual support extends far beyond just translation. For example, you can localize content for different states in the United States without any translation. For any international or ethnic localization, however, internationalization support with the DAM system *may* be a requirement.

Internationalization enables users to access the system in different languages. If all your users work with the DAM system in only one language, such as French, you need internationalization support, and the user interface would present text, help text, and error messages in French. We would also expect that the metadata could be entered and presented in the chosen language and could be searched in the chosen language, returning properly sorted result sets. This is a property of the search engine, of course, and not of the user interface.

If, however, you need users to access the asset management system in different languages, such as Spanish and English, you need a system that supports both internationalization and simultaneously multilingual metadata. Furthermore, to support multinational or multilingual access, you require a process for converting or adding language-specific metadata for the assets that are available in each language.

In all localization efforts regardless of region, you need to establish specific workflows that define the localization process steps and examine how the DAM system can support them.

We see at least two major implications for your DAM effort:

1. To support multinational or multilingual access, you require a process for converting or adding language-specific metadata.

2. You need to establish localization workflows and determine how the DAM system supports them.

Localization Features

Unlike WCM support for localization, a DAM system also has to address the need to support the preparation of assets for various channels or media types, such as print, Web, video, PDF, or image. The system needs to support the following:

- Versions and configurations of assets, and be able to tag them appropriately for regional access and use

- Conversion, transformation, or transcoding features to format assets for the targeted channel

- Internationalization (optional)

- Multilingual metadata (optional)

- Multilingual search (optional)

Internationalization Features

If you are deploying the DAM system or providing access to it across multiple countries or languages, the software itself may need to support multiple languages and dialects. The system should provide an entire experience in the language. Specifically, the system should present all screens, menus and labels, help text, and error messages in the language of choice. Any text entry fields—particularly those for metadata—should handle the language, and the underlying search engine must be able to index, sort, and return results in an order appropriate to the language. Lastly, with respect to the user interface, the system must present the textual information well and appropriately regardless of language or the orientation require-ments—left to right versus right to left—of the language.

Transformation and Transcoding

A DAM system must prepare, assemble, or reassemble assets and then deliver those assets, metadata, or both to various outlets or media in the appropriate formats. Transformation refers to the system's capability to transform images to another format, and transcoding refers to the changing or encoding of video from one format to another.

In addition to transforming or transcoding an asset for delivery to various channels, assembly includes many forms of automated asset preparation:

- On-the-fly use of transformation and transcoding capabilities in accordance with user- defined or system-provided parameters

- Any automated assembly or reassembly

- Watermark images or video frames

- Compression of a file or files into archive formats such as ZIP or TAR for more compact delivery

- Digital rights management (DRM) encryption

- Metadata transformation

- Metadata insertion or write-back

On-the-Fly Conversions

On-the-fly use of transformation and transcoding capabilities is the most common automated assembly feature. It allows you to create and deliver, usually immediately, an asset that has changed in format, size, resolution, scale, encoding, or bit rate. The DAM system allows you to select the parameters or use a predefined named set of parameters (see Figure 6.4). Some systems run this process as a structured workflow, providing an additional level of automation and control over the whole assembly and delivery process.

Some systems queue requests for conversions and perform them asynchronously. This method suits video transcoding, which can take significant time, depending on the original and target file formats and video length. Systems that provide asynchronous conversions typically use a status monitor and notification mechanism to let you track the process to completion. These notifications may be via email or through a display within the DAM application. They may be active or passive, which requires that you check to see if the process is completed. Be sure to look into these aspects of asset conversion.

○	**Apply Watermark To Image** *Applies a selected image as a watermark* *to an image*	psd, jpg, gif, png, tif
○	**Auto Levels** *Automatically adjust levels in an image*	psd, jpg, gif, png, tif
○	**Change Resolution** *Allows the user to change the DPI for* *images*	psd, jpg, gif, png, tif
○	**Change the ICC Color Profile** *Allows the user to specify the ICC Color* *Profile for images*	psd, jpg, gif, png, tif
○	**Convert Image Format** *Converts an image from one format to* *another specified image format*	psd, jpg, gif, png, tif, bmp, pnm, pgm, ppm, pbm, wbmp, pcx, pct, tga, sgi, sct, jp2
○	**Convert Images to PDF** *Converts images to PDF*	pcf
○	**Embed Metadata** *Embed metadata from object in image* *properties*	jpg
○	**Extract Properties** *Adds image properties to object* *metadata*	jpg
○	**Flips an Image** *Flip an image horizontally or vertically*	psd, jpg, gif, png, tif
○	**Resize Image** *Resizes an image with a specified height* *and/or width*	psd, jpg, gif, png, tif, bmp, pnm, pgm, ppm, pbm, wbmp, pcx, pct, tga, sgi, sct, jp2
○	**Resize Image - Preserve Aspect Ratio** *Resizes an image while preserving the* *proportion of height and width*	psd, jpg, gif, png, tif, bmp, pnm, pgm, ppm, pbm, wbmp, pcx, pct, tga, sgi, sct, jp2

FIGURE 6.4
Transformation options in EMC Documentum Digital Asset Manager.

Some DAM systems provide deeper image-rendering support:

- Composing images from multiple pieces. Take a price, a starburst-shaped design, the text "Sale Price," and an image of a product and compose a new picture that depicts the text "Sale Price: $299.00," set inside the starburst layered on top of the product. Historically, these images have been manually created through labor-intensive design processes. Some systems can automate this process.

- Visible watermarking.

- Producing contact sheets that include specific metadata beneath each photo. Some imaging engines used for on-the-fly processing have template-based generation of composite images and can create this kind of contact sheet.

Compound Asset Assembly in DAM

The DAM system can automate the preparation of compound assets, such as QuarkXPress or Adobe InDesign layout files, PowerPoint decks, and potentially video files. Most systems can regenerate a layout document if it has been broken down and stored as pieces. Typically, they generate a PDF file of the layout file for delivery. Some systems perform this on ingestion and store the PDF as a preview or proxy rendition; the reason is that most users don't have the layout software on their machines and thus are unable to view or review the document. Other systems can perform it in assembly prior to delivery, especially if the systems support modification of the compound asset.

For those systems that support breaking up of PowerPoint files into individual slides, you can rebuild the deck or create a new deck from selected slides as an assembly capability. Some systems also support generating PDF and Flash versions of the presentation. Both PDF and Flash versions are secure, nonmodifiable forms of the PowerPoint presentation. PDF versions do not retain any animation or slide transitions, whereas Flash does. However, in today's tablet-based and mobile world, with the rise of HTML5 and responsive design, the need for Flash-based file conversions and delivery has lessened substantially.

Watermarking

Some workflows call for the release of only watermarked instances of images or videos; others require that the video must have a visible "bug" on one of the corners. Adding a watermark is a kind of asset assembly. There are two kinds of watermarking: visible and embedded. Visible watermarks typically overlie the image, fundamentally altering its composition and identity. Invisible watermarks are woven into the file in a technically advanced manner to avoid removal but aid detection by other hardware and software. Enterprises use watermarks to provide forensic traceability for high-value materials. Digimarc and Verance are two leading providers of digital watermarking, particularly for images, audio, and video files.

Don't confuse watermarking with encryption or DRM. It's strictly a means of embedding an identifying marker inside a file, usually in a stealthy manner, so that the source or copyright ownership of the file can be traced later if necessary.

File Compression

Assets can be very large. It's common to want to download a bunch of smaller assets all at once in only one file. Many DAM products support compressing a file or files into a single archive-formatted file such as ZIP, StuffIt, or TAR, for more compact and efficient delivery. The systems vary, however, in which of these formats they support.

DRM Encryption

As an additional measure of security, you may need or want to deliver your assets in DRM-enabled containers. DRM allows you to better control asset access and proliferation once outside the DAM system. An increasing number of enterprises use it for video and audio information and sensitive corporate assets. Many vendors provide DRM as an optional integration point to the system. In many cases, the vendor has partnered with a DRM provider or integrated with one of the few DRM vendors, such as Irdeto, Microsoft, or Adobe.

Metadata Export and Transformation

Users often want externally consumable forms of metadata. Most systems support the ability to export metadata. Some enable you to control the export and provide the metadata that accompanies a list of assets in specific formats, such as in XML or an Excel spreadsheet, or to a specified format (such as for Amazon or iTunes).

Metadata Insertion or Write-back

Related to metadata transformation, you may want to write back the metadata directly into the file in a standard metadata format such as XMP, IPTC, and EXIF. This embedded metadata can facilitate downstream processing on the assets.

Multichannel Delivery

Delivery includes the ability to deliver assets, metadata, or both to users, devices, and locations. Delivery implicitly includes the integration to external technologies or systems that facilitate the actual delivery. Most DAM systems provide interfaces to the basic ones, such as email, FTP, and download, out of the box. You may need system customization or additional integration for video delivery, delivery through new and emerging WAN optimization or secure delivery technology, and delivery to tablet and mobile devices.

While broadcasters have traditionally delivered over satellite, cable, and on-air TV, multiplatform delivery more commonly refers to publishing audio/video assets on the Web and to mobile phones. The format and the resolution needed for on-air, the Web, and for mobile are all different.

Increasingly, broadcasters want to make content that aired on TV available on the Web and on mobile devices. While this approach is not ideal, many of them reuse the same version that was aired on TV as on the Web. Even this requires converting videos into a format that's friendly for the Web. The same is true for mobile; that is, the content needs to be formatted for mobile devices. More sophisticated broadcasters want to tailor content to take advantage of user behaviors of the respective platforms, as well as unique features (for example, can it insert clickable ads?). While specialized software generally takes care of video transcoding for its respective platforms, broadcast-oriented DAM software plays a key role in publishing workflows for multiplatform delivery.

Mobile Applications

Increasingly, vendors are releasing a subset of DAM functionality—particularly workflow management—through native applications for the iPad and iPhone. Using streaming server software, the video is streamed on these mobile devices so that users can preview the content during workflow approvals. Notifications related to approvals and exception handling are also delivered.

Broadcast, media-oriented DAM products also support remote news and sports reporting use cases through add-on modules. With these tools, live feeds from the field can be fed into the newsroom for broadcast.

DAM packages that offer robust transformation and transcoding are able to meet the following criteria:

- Varied file types or previews/thumbnails can be previewed in the search results.

- Previews and thumbnails are automatically produced on asset ingest, a process that is easily configured. The DAM system uses portals or engines to improve capabilities.

- The product can transcode or transform hundreds of file types, and the processes can be automated.

Personalization

Another level of configuration is personalization. We define personalization as the ability to tailor the user's DAM experience on an individual or group basis.

The user experience has two facets: what they can *see* and what they can *do*. Users can affect their experience, or the system can affect the users' experience. Given this, let's consider the three primary forms of personalization.

Preferences-Based Personalization

With preferences-based personalization, users indicate their preferences (usually during an initial session) and refine them at various times. What they can see or do tracks with the tasks they need to accomplish. These preferences tailor the user interface and each user's workspace. They might include defining how many and what size preview thumbnail images will be displayed on a page or which folders are automatically opened in the folder hierarchy. They may also include predefined filters or a user's own saved-search criteria, so the system can quickly execute common queries and filter result sets or pages. Further, users can control metadata visibility, so the system displays only the desired metadata about an asset in brief or detailed views.

In some systems, users can control what assets they share in an ad hoc manner with other users. They can establish private folders or workspaces of invited participants and define their own folder hierarchies with their naming convention within the private workspace. They may also be able to set notification controls on structured workflows they're involved with, defining what kinds of notification they receive and how much notification. For example, they could receive notification of new or changed assets or assets requiring review or approval. In these private workspaces, the system assigns a user name and password to each user for authentication. The system commonly uses stored personal profiles, which users can access as needed.

Role-Based Personalization

Another approach is predefined groups (also called *role-based personalization*). In this model, the system categorizes users into predetermined groups or roles. A role determines which assets a user can see and access, which operations or actions a user of that role can take, and potentially which other users that user can share or communicate with within the system. Depending on the role, the administrator enables or disables certain features or functions. For example, when a user of a particular role logs in, that user will find that certain menu items, actions, filters, shared-saved searches, and other capabilities have been removed or grayed out.

Additionally, certain assets, versions, folders, and metadata will be inaccessible and invisible. Role-based personalization allows the administrator to control who can see and do what, to keep users focused on their tasks and roles.

Brand-Based Delivery: Look and Appearance

In some systems, the user interface appearance—its look and feel, graphics, skins, or colors—may also be tied to the role. Or it may be tied to other constructs, such as the location in the directory structure where you log in. This allows the system to appear differently to different groups of users. We call this *brand-based customization*. Consider a pharmaceutical company that has multiple drug brands or a manufacturing company that has multiple product lines. Depending on which brand or product line you're affiliated with, you log in to the system, and you see the colors, logos, and graphics tailored to the brand. Enterprises also can use this feature to segment different departments or to brand the experience of external users such as distributors or partners.

CHAPTER 7

DAM Technology Services: Architecture and Administration

Now that you're familiar with the various features that enable the end-to-end creation and distribution of assets, let's explore the different aspects of system administration and management—the parts that allow you to configure and manage how the systems work.

Application Development and System Administration

DAM systems offer different levels of facilities for application development and system administration. We'll look at these facilities broadly, evaluating vendors based on overall offerings for the administrator and developer, and then look into the detailed functions within these services.

The core of media-oriented, broadcast-caliber DAM software comprises a set of server software that performs a wide variety of services: essence management, video analysis, workflow management, indexing and search, integrations, and system administration tasks. Broadcast DAM systems are also expected to handle vast amounts of rich media content; thus, the underlying architecture determines scalability and performance.

Configuration and customization differ substantially. While you can enhance and tailor a system with both, configuration specifies predefined changes that have been built in to the system, do not require coding, and can be performed by an administrator. With customization, you enhance the system by adding new capabilities, applications, or system integrations that require programming. Extension and integration are specialized forms of customization.

System Security

The DAM system's security model defines, organizes, and manages users and their abilities within the DAM. It controls what they can see and do, which objects (such as files and metadata) they can perform actions on, and where and when they can do something in the DAM application.

Many people can be involved in asset creation, management, production, and consumption. A DAM system facilitates these processes and provides access directly to asset creators, editors, reviewers, and users. A system installation often leads to more people becoming involved in these processes. To manage internal access and privileges, you need a system that scales to support a variety of different user types and the expansion of the user base. Finally, you also need to secure the content itself.

Let's dig into these issues in more detail.

Access Control

The DAM system enforces security primarily through access control. As with any technology application, access control has several pieces:

- **Authentication:** Proving that you are who you say you are, typically by providing a user name and password. A check typically is done against a directory service like an LDAP or Active Directory server.

- **Authorization:** Identifying what "entitlements" you do or do not have, based on your Directory record, specific rights granted in the DAM, or both.

Authentication and Authorization

Most DAM packages provide both authentication and authorization mechanisms. Many can tie into existing corporate directory systems, such as LDAP or Active Directory servers, for basic authentication. Authorization occurs within the DAM itself.

Note that authentication and authorization methods vary markedly among products. For example, some products access an LDAP repository in real time. Others require that the LDAP server sync with—or cache—credentials within the product's access control lists on a regular schedule. In the former case, you need to ensure the complete reliability of the network between your asset management system and your directory server. In the latter case, there can be periods when a user's rights have been expunged in the corporate directory, but the user still has access to the asset management system's privileges, or conversely, when a user has been added to the corporate directory but isn't visible to the DAM system until the next synchronization. Beyond these timing concerns, there are other issues with directory services, including whether the system can support the creation of new users when they are added to the LDAP server and how to do this.

Single Sign-On

In some enterprises, the IT department insists that users have a
single login for all the applications they can access. In this case, the
DAM system may need to support single sign-on (SSO) and integrate
with specific SSO devices and systems. You almost certainly need
some customization here (see Figure 7.1).

FIGURE 7.1
Creating a role and assigning privileges in AssetBank to support single sign-on
and to integrate with specific SSO devices and systems.

Roles and Groups

The DAM system can assign privileges to users based on the role
they play—their place and job in the workflow—or the group to
which they belong. These privileges define their authority; the scope
and visibility of the asset population they can access; and typically
the set of functions, operations, or capabilities they have rights to
perform. Often, a user makes up a group of one. Note, however, that
some vendors do not have notions of groups in their system. Others
have groups but not roles.

Consider the following groups and roles for a generic enterprise.

- **Salespeople:** Can only view and download assets

- **Marketing managers:** Can upload assets, add metadata, initiate and manage reviews, approve assets, and control visibility and distribution of assets

- **Graphic designers:** Can create, modify, and submit for approval images and layout files (may also be a role)

- **Librarians:** Can manage classification systems and metadata vocabularies

Sample Roles

- **Super user:** Can perform any function in the system

- **Editor:** Approves assets

- **Author:** Submits assets

- **Reviewer:** Reviews assets

- **Intern:** Adds metadata to assets

- **Consumer:** Downloads and consumes assets

- **External partner:** Can consume visible assets but not deposit assets

You may need a system that lets you use a combination of groups and roles. Using preceding samples, let's say that Suzanne serves as an editor in the marketing managers group. She initiates review processes and approves the changes or updates that authors have made to assets.

Some products ship with generic roles already configured for your use. Except in the very low-end systems, you can modify those roles as necessary. Not all applications, however, allow you to create completely new roles. Among those that offer this capability, you may not be able to circumscribe functions exactly how you would like. For example, you may want your interns to add and modify metadata but have no other privileges, or you may need your managers to initiate workflow tasks but not be able to author content.

Additionally, some systems use a combination of privileges and permissions to set entitlements. Privileges correspond to what a user has the right to do. Objects, such as an asset or folder, grant permissions, allowing a given operation to be performed on them. For example, a user may have permission to modify an asset, but if the asset does not allow modification, the user cannot perform the action. The user must get consent from the asset owner to perform the specific operation. This combination may sound attractive to you and may in fact become necessary in highly sensitive environments. In reality, however, the attendant complexity frequently becomes an administrative nightmare and major support problem, as users are locked out of certain assets and they don't know why.

Given this wide variance in the implementation of the security models, make this a point of emphasis when speaking with prospective vendors. You should be sure to understand how to set up the roles and groups you think you need and the granularity of control offered by the security model. Consider the complexity and power offered by the product and your expected use case. If, for example, you have very simple needs, stay cautious about products that offer highly granular control mechanisms (which may include things like hierarchical roles). These mechanisms can be hard to manage, and a novice administrator can accidentally create problems, such as locking various roles out of functions or assets to which they should really have access. This is also an excellent area to explore in reference calls or site visits.

Asset Security: Encryption

Asset management systems may offer additional security features beyond access control. Depending on the nature of the files or the value of assets or metadata, a DAM system might offer one or more flavors of encryption.

For some companies, assets represent critical or sensitive intellectual property (IP). Certain brand assets, such as a movie that is digitally distributed, military photos, a sensitive financial or brand strategy document, or sensitive metadata, should not be allowed to be modified. In all of these cases, you may want additional levels of security beyond access control. Furthermore, many companies using a SaaS provider need to encrypt assets or metadata transmitted to and from the hosted facility.

Encryption can be found in three places in the DAM system:

- Import or upload

- Storage

- Delivery or download

Some IT organizations or implementations may need to encrypt files as they're transferred from the user's desktop to the system, particularly for SaaS-provided DAM systems. Furthermore, when the SaaS vendor implements the system as a shared repository and service, you may prefer to encrypt requests for additional security and privacy. The reverse is also desirable: encrypting assets to transfer from the asset management system to the end location (for example, desktop, FTP site, or email).

Asset management systems commonly use SSL for over-the-wire encryption, but you may encounter other protocols and approaches. For example, many video formats adhere to various video-industry encryption standards, and SOAP payloads can be digitally signed and encrypted. Remember that SSL adds extra overhead to a wire transfer, however, and can slow delivery.

Alternatively, you can apply digital rights management to distribute sensitive assets, files, or purchased content such as books or music. Broadcast-oriented, media-centric vendors usually tell you to use the DRM technology from the content provider rather than providing any DRM services of their own. Note that DRM differs from the rights management discussed earlier. DRM enforces access and use, based on the dictated rights, rather than simply specifying the rights and privileges. With DRM, the asset and its metadata reside in a secure, encrypted envelope. Only those who have the proper keys have rights to access it after download or distribution.

In some systems, XMP metadata can be inserted into images prior to transmission or download, and individual fields can be encrypted. This function allows the metadata to travel with the asset. It facilitates automated downstream processing on the asset, while protecting sensitive fields from tampering, access, or change. This is an emerging area of metadata encryption and an emerging area of DAM technology. Instead of maintaining the metadata separate from the asset, as when it is in a repository, the system embeds the metadata into the asset, providing a true "asset" that can provide much deeper information about itself to external systems.

Finally, some highly secure DAM systems (primarily for government and military uses) may require encryption of assets and metadata in the repository, that is, a managed file system. This type of system requires encrypting both the database and repository and is less common in commercial use.

With any encryption/decryption use, performance and visibility are primary issues. Both encryption and decryption add overhead to the transmission and manipulation of assets. Assets must be encrypted before transmission, decrypted afterward, and decrypted prior to manipulation and use. These operations clearly can slow down performance; SSL is an example. For larger assets or a batch load of a large number of assets, encryption can slow delivery. You encounter the issue of visibility when you upload ZIP archives as assets. In this case, the DAM system treats the ZIP file asset as it does any other file format. It may not be able to provide an icon for the ZIP file asset and may not be able to provide a preview. In those rare cases with encrypted databases *and* repositories, access control governs the asset's visibility. If you have proper access to an asset, the system would likely decrypt and present it for you. This process, however, adds overhead to the display performance.

Common Technologies

The underlying code base (that is, the programming languages in which the software is developed) is different among the various DAM products. Many are .NET based and run on the Microsoft technology stack; others combine a mix of technologies like Java, C, and C++ for different underlying modules.

Many DAM systems today use Microsoft SQL Server as the data repository, but those that are more broadcast-oriented and media-focused run on IBM DB2 or Oracle database software. Search functionality is implemented using Lucene or the related Solr and Elasticsearch technology (both are open source). Most DAM systems run on Windows, Linux, or UNIX operating systems.

If your enterprise has corporate standards about the technology on which the product is built (versus just being interested in the system's performance, maintainability, and scalability), these differences are important considerations.

Reporting and Analytics

With the increasing maturity of the DAM marketplace, buyers now look at the software not just for asset management and workflow automation, but for real management. Management begs metrics—and metrics require reports. Ironically, many digital asset management systems don't provide such reports, although some vendors are waking up to the fact that they should. Some systems don't even create logs upon which you could build such reports. Look back over your business objectives and figure out how your system could help you to measure how you're doing. Decide which ones are most important for your business.

Here is a small sampling of reports that could help you justify the asset management system's value and expand its adoption and use:

- Who is logging in to the system, how often, and who does not use it at all?

- Which assets are most frequently downloaded or emailed?

- Which assets are most frequently viewed or accessed?

- How has the number of assets grown in volume over time?

- Who is contributing assets and who is consuming them?

- How many of each kind of asset do you have?

- Are there any orphaned assets?

- What volumes and types of content have been classified according to specific nodes in your taxonomy or by community tagging?

- How much storage is consumed?

- What payment or usage obligations have been incurred?

- Are there any "rogue" assets in the system?

- What are all the derivatives or linked assets?

You may also want to produce reports in various formats or utilize existing third-party reporting tools that you already have in-house. Some DAMs support third-party tools, allowing you to generate more configurable or custom reports in various formats, such as Excel, Word, or PDF.

Distribution

A key aspect of scalability and capacity is technology distribution. In this context, we don't mean the assembly and delivery of the assets themselves, rather the extent to which and how a system can logically and physically distribute services and repositories.

We see three major opportunities in this area:

- Distributing services vertically by emphasizing load on the client, server, or storage tiers.

- Distributing services horizontally by separating services, perhaps putting very intensive services, such as transcoding, on specially configured hardware, or clustering services for better performance. We return to this discussion in the next section on scaling.

- Distributing the repository for potentially better access and performance.

Distribution describes where the processing, storage, business logic, and aspects of the user experience occur in the system. These capabilities may be centralized or distributed—or some combination of both, depending on the level at which you look. Distribution is a function of the overall architecture and is governed by architectural design decisions. As an architectural issue, it fundamentally affects several aspects of the overall system, including scalability and capacity, resource allocation, and hardware and software costs. As such, it has a significant effect on your total cost of ownership. Depending on the architecture, you may be able to add hardware incrementally, improving your system's performance, capacity, or geographic distribution at a reasonable cost. However, you may have to replicate the entire structure to achieve your performance, capacity, or distribution goals.

Asset management systems are complex software systems that integrate a variety of components to provide digital asset management services. A DAM system has to upload, render, process, store, index, manage, search, transform, secure, and deliver assets and metadata. Where it performs these functions is the primary issue affecting how well the system performs.

Many DAM vendors have adopted service-oriented architecture (SOA) principles where different functions and processing services are clearly separated, with well-documented interfaces (inputs and outputs of a service) to each other. SOA principles make the software modular and make for easier maintenance as well. Another advantage is the ability to deploy multiple instances of the same service on either the same server or a different server. This enables you to start small and add more capacity as requirements grow. Of course, your site's hardware configuration is determined in combination with other system needs, but generally speaking, a well-architected SOA system that can run on commodity software is a viable approach.

While we've mainly discussed the software aspects, many DAM systems are designed to run on commodity hardware. (Commodity hardware refers to Wintel, or Windows servers with Intel chips, which cost less compared to higher-end servers from Oracle and others.) Google has popularized this approach, and instead of using a small number of high-end servers, it uses a larger number of less powerful computers, thus easily adding incremental capacity at lower costs and providing better failover support.

Asset management systems vary significantly in architecture. Key areas of differentiation include where distribution functions perform, how the components or subsystems perform these functions and work together, and how these functions can scale as systems grow in capacity and utilization. Most DAM systems use a centralized model. In this model, the system transfers and uploads files to a central location for processing and storage. This model generally works for small- to medium-sized files. For large and very large video files and print-ready PDF files, however, this approach may be problematic, especially if your enterprise has multiple geographic locations attempting to access these files. You don't want to move them around very much—if at all.

The system must process every asset to generate one or more renditions. Rendition examples include a thumbnail image; streamable, low-resolution proxies for video; or PDF files representing a rendered preview form of a brochure. Again, for small to medium files, this process works well in a centralized location. This central location could have a farm of media processing engines distributed over multiple local machines. For longer or for HD videos, the system should process them locally to the user, perhaps store them locally, and hand up the resulting proxies to the system for centralized storage.

Even if the system appears to be centralized from an access perspective or a logical view, it may physically distribute the storage. In this case, the system allows assets to live in multiple geographic locations while maintaining a centralized index of the assets. It may use a variety of technologies to do this, including distributed databases or distributed computing technologies, such as CORBA, Java Message Service (JMS), or Microsoft .NET.

Systems vary on where the DAM application runs. Client/server applications provide rich functionality as desktop applications that communicate with a back-end server. Other (and today, most) systems are browser-based, executing on the server, and serving the pieces from a Web or application server to the user via a thin client. Increasingly, more highly interactive and responsive rich Internet applications—using Web development technologies like HTML5 and JavaScript—provide desktop-like functionality and interactivity in a browser, and execute the business logic or application in specialized servers.

In short, an asset management system integrates many processing capabilities from various places. Most business organizations couldn't care less about these architectural issues. However, they are critical to your IT group, which will have to manage the system and its infrastructure.

We recommend examining several key issues:

- How the processing and storage are distributed
- Whether each tier of processing can be scaled independently, thereby reducing overall costs, allowing you to spend only where necessary
- Whether local processing is needed or desirable
- How the storage scales
- What communication mechanisms are used to enable distributed processing
- Whether it uses an application server, web server, or some other technology, and how these can be clustered and scaled for performance and capacity

You need to weigh manageability, flexibility, and power against the needs of your workflows and users' geographic locales.

Configuration

Configuration means changing some comparatively simple default settings, often through a browser interface or by editing a text- or XML-based config file. Adding users to and removing them from a system represents a common, and usually simple, configuration. Others can be more complex, yet by our definition, configuration does not require a developer.

A broad range of capabilities can be configurable. Beyond the typical system-tuning parameters for the core repository, database, DAM application or application server, you can usually configure the following:

- Metadata schema

- Folder name and structures

- Metadata presentation—what metadata is visible on which screens

- Definitions of user roles and groups and their privileges

- Structured workflows—who, what, when, and how frequently (often using templates)

- File types

- Predefined transformations and renditions

- Filters and predefined saved searches

- Log contents

- Initial landing pages

- The user interface appearance, or "skin"

In some cases, the metadata model requires SQL coding to define the model, making it more of a customization than a configuration. Additionally, DAM systems vary in their support of single sign-on and integration with and access to information in existing directory structures such as LDAP or Microsoft Active Directory. In some, this process can be configured; others require programming.

ALERT

While broad configuration facilities can be attractive to the business user wanting to modify a system, they also can get you into trouble. You may encounter tools that have little or no formal settings management and no way to automatically roll back changes or test new configurations in a test environment. In the end, you still need proper configuration management policies and training to use these services. For this reason, configuration facilities often end up simplifying the developer's job, rather than empowering the nontechnical businessperson.

Customization, Integration, and Extensibility

Customization means writing some custom code to do something that a browser-based configurator couldn't accomplish. One of your first considerations here should be configuration management.

Just what might need to be customized? In a DAM system, customization can apply to virtually any part of the system. Enterprises commonly customize unavailable features or integration with external systems. Occasionally, the user interface requires customization to make it more approachable or to tailor it to a specific use case or workflow. You may need to write code to modify or add workflow actions; to integrate with an unsupported media processing engine, tool, or application; or to integrate with a back-end accounting or billing system.

Some systems have APIs or better-designed development APIs. The vendors set up these APIs so that third parties and IT shops can extend the system with minimal training. Beware of systems that appear to have tremendous function in the vendor demo. It's not that the system can't do these things; it's just that vendors may glue together many examples of previously customized capabilities that are not actually available out of the box. Adding these capabilities will result in additional cost to you. Be sure to ask whether a specific feature is native or if it is a customization.

Customization also can get you into trouble. Poorly written code can cause memory or security leaks. You can encounter thorny problems at upgrade or patch time. You may need to retest the code against the new DAM system and possibly rewrite it if it doesn't work properly.

Make sure any code is well documented—we recommend requiring this as a condition of payment—and follow best practices laid out by your vendor. If your vendor doesn't lay out best practices and you expect to perform significant customization, reconsider your choice of tools.

As in customizing, "extending" software requires coding, but typically at a deeper level. Extension deals with creating discrete objects, classes, or modules that run inside or alongside the system.

You would extend a DAM product to supply features that might be missing entirely, such as a personalization subsystem, workflow subsystem, report writer, archive, or a different display of metadata or assets. All of these caveats still apply, that is, the importance of configuration management. You should pay close attention to possible security conflicts with the system itself. You also may encounter potential problems if you mess around with lower-level application or platform settings.

In the vendor evaluations, when we say a product is more "platform oriented" rather than "product oriented," we mean that it lends itself better to extension, potentially at the expense of implementation speed and ease.

Integrating your DAM with other applications or infrastructure will require a combination of configurations, customizations, and extensions. For more high-definition scenarios, broadcasters have a plethora of systems, and you will need to engage in an elaborate dance between two or more different systems. Broadcast-oriented systems can integrate with a variety of systems for media processing, delivery, monetization, rights management, and video system infrastructure.

At the easy end of the spectrum is data integration, in which you integrate information from another repository or system. Some DAM products have mechanisms to draw metadata from outside their own repository. Of course, this process can be complicated, especially with respect to synchronization, security, and versioning. You need to respect the business logic of both systems when moving and accessing data. Work through an API wherever possible.

Process integration can be more complicated for two reasons. First, most DAM systems do not have sophisticated event models. Second, our industry has not standardized as effectively around business process integration approaches. You may want to look for supported, prepackaged connectors between systems rather than writing your own.

Note that, unlike enterprise portal software, most DAM systems were not originally designed as integration platforms. Historically, the DAM industry has largely supported freestanding digital asset management operations. This is starting to change, but packaged software tends to change more slowly than business needs. For better or for worse, most larger enterprises still look to portal or business process management (BPM) software as their core information integration platform.

As you get a feel for your intended use of the DAM and work your way through the features and capabilities of prospective products, determine where you'll have to customize the system to fit the needs of your workflow and use cases and where the vendor provides built-in avenues to configure the system. Configuration is significantly cheaper and can be very flexible.

Scalability and Performance

Scalability and *high performance* are words that vendors love to use; IT needs to understand them. Digital asset management systems can range from single-user desktop applications to full-blown enterprise software systems. You need to examine how vendors portray the scalability, reliability, and capacity of their offerings.

Scalability deals with how you can expand or contract the system in response to increases or decreases in the number of users, assets, simultaneous operations, or execution of structured workflow processes. It also relates to how the system uses hardware, CPUs, storage, and networking infrastructure.

Reliability measures the system's resilience, uptime, and consistency of operation. Can it use RAID arrays for redundancy and failover? Is it fault tolerant? Does it support clustering? Does it run on top of standard application server platforms that can themselves be scaled according to commonly understood approaches? Or is it a freestanding service that must be scaled according to vendor-prescribed means?

Capacity measures a variety of functions, including maximum processing, throughput, number of users, number of assets, and trans-mission speed, at a given time. Is the DAM system efficient in its use of hardware, or is it resource intensive? Is it multithreaded or multi-CPU?

In addition to the hardware and software considerations dis-cussed here, another important aspect is the design of the network between the DAM system and user desktops. Because we're talking about large volumes of video assets, the network bandwidth must accommodate a large volume of network traffic. If users work on low-resolution proxies and export EDLs instead of actual assets, it will reduce network traffic.

All of these issues must be considered and depend on the anticipated use and adoption of the system, IT's predisposition to managing and maintaining the infrastructure, and the total cost of ownership.

Caching

The ability to cache information fundamentally speeds performance. Caching can affect system performance in several areas in a DAM system, primarily by serving as a place for system components to store and retrieve frequently or recently used data, assets, or information. The caching capability, however, may not be considered as a critical component.

In fact, you will find that caching is generally treated as a "tuning parameter" in most DAM systems. It can potentially be tuned at several places in the system, depending on the DAM's architecture. For example, if the DAM system uses a commercial database, you can tune the database cache for more optimal query performance and result set management. If, on the other hand, the DAM uses an application server as a fundamental part of its architecture, you can tune the application server's execution cache or data cache for different performance profiles. Depending on the transcoding technology used, the system may or may not provide and utilize a cache. If the system provides a cache, it can speed repetitive transformation or rendering operations on the same asset by retrieving it from the cache instead of processing it again. If the DAM makes use of a web server, you may be able to tweak the presentation performance of web pages in Web-based DAM applications.

In general, you should determine the DAM system's capability for tuning performance. However, beware that caching is a very sophisticated topic and takes a true expert to understand all of its nuances. If you'll be dealing in large volumes of assets or very *large* assets, you should have a knowledgeable person assess the system's capabilities before assuming that it can do whatever the salesperson promises it can do.

DAM Administration

DAM systems provide tools for administrators to configure the DAM instance and monitoring tools. Administrators monitor both the status of the software services (running or stopped) and the status of different workflow tasks (for example, file transfers and format conversions). Among the different DAM vendors, these monitoring tools range from basic and utilitarian to extensive and polished.

Administrator User Interface

The last topic we discuss is the user interface and interaction, but it's foremost in users' minds as they evaluate tools and you persuade your colleagues to fully embrace your DAM system. There are two separate aspects of the user experience. The first is the asset manager's user experience, and the second is the administrator's user experience, which is often neglected or deemed less important. Given the modern emphasis of configuration over customization with software products, the usability of the administrator interface cannot be overlooked.

As previously mentioned, the DAM toolset consists of both browser-based and decreasingly, Windows-based clients. In the early years of DAM (mid to late 1990s), users had to be familiar with many different tools, each for accomplishing a specific set of tasks. Increasingly, however, DAM vendors are focused on combining multiple, disparate tools into a more tightly unified toolset in an effort to provide the required functionality all in one place.

Currently, users can navigate workspaces (folders with assets), search for assets, examine the details of those assets, preview assets, and change assets all from a single interface. Despite these improvements, the DAM user interface can overwhelm users because multiple screens are trying to capture as much rich detail about assets as possible. To prevent cognitive overload, it is important to map users to specific roles and display only UI screens that are relevant to the role. DAM vendors support role-based access to functionality and features, and during the initial rollout, the UI is configured to support different types of roles.

Many DAM vendors provide the ability to apply visual themes and skins to the DAM user interface, and some options are configured by the administrator and some by the user. Dark-colored and light-hued themes are available based on where the users are working; some users work in dark broadcast rooms and would prefer darker-colored themes. In general, these customization options are limited, and DAM products generally don't offer a wide variety of choice.

In theory, the user interface of the DAM product could be easily localized from a technical point of view, but DAM vendors' support for UI localizations varies. In general, European languages (which follow the same left-to-right orientation as English) tend to be better supported than Asian languages.

Rich media is largely visual, and as such, it needs to be seen and experienced to be understood. Thus, the presentation and usability of the user interface and the system's seamless ability to integrate with content creation and visualization tools are essential for establishing a rich and effective experience.

Describing user interfaces and the user interaction in words is difficult. Therefore, we use the following figures to help you visualize and understand some of the key features that are important. See the example shown in Figure 7.2.

FIGURE 7.2
Annotating images in globaledit allows photographers and creative users to make comments, annotations, and markup directly in context.

Most DAM UIs have a common set of features:

- A tree structure for visualizing the folder or collection hierarchy and browsing

- An asset overview display providing thumbnails and possibly animated GIFs and summary metadata representing the content of the currently opened folder

- Icons that depict various additional information, state, or rankings on each asset

- Actions depicted as icons for functions that can be performed on individual or groups of assets

- A menu structure for additional functionality beyond the current screen

- Detailed asset and metadata views

- Search fields and search result pages

- Mechanisms for selecting assets, such as check boxes, drag-and-drop functionality clip-bins, and shopping carts

- Metadata entry fields

To become a power user with these features requires training and frequent system use. Indeed, while these UI features are common, the quality of a user's experience derives from the ease of organization, flow, and user interactivity in performing tasks. You won't be able to evaluate these features without trying the product first-hand, against your own workflows and scenarios (see Figure 7.3).

FIGURE 7.3
Asset management system UIs typically have a tree structure type of navigation that allows you to browse through assets by topic and view thumbnails of assets within each category (called a "library" or sometimes a "job"), as depicted here in Extensis Portfolio.

You may want to consider several other UI aspects:

- **Organization:** Is information laid out intelligently? Are the features to access and work with the information intuitive so that you can perform your job effectively?

- **Presentation of metadata:** Can the metadata be configured? By you? By the administrator? For different roles or groups? How much control do you have over hiding metadata or showing a summary of fields of your choice?

- **Personalization of the UI:** Can you manipulate the display of the UI to see only what you need or want to see? Does it change based on your role? Do you have any control over how and what you want to display?

- **Ability to easily perform the task you need:** How does the UI flow for a given task? Does it take a single step or several steps? Is it intuitive? Does it help you to do your job?

- **Screen refresh and performance:** How much time do you wait between each screen refresh? Does it only refresh regions of the screen that need it?

On this last point, more modern user interface technologies such as HTML5 have significantly improved user interface interactivity, performance, responsiveness, and usability. Newer web application development technologies enable you to update smaller regions of the screen, versus the old, page-based world of click-and-wait. This optimization can provide both greater interactivity and increased responsiveness, resulting in a significantly better user experience. Faceted search endeavors to bring such interactive experiences to the search functionality as well.

Many DAM vendors have made significant investments in integrating with the more common creation tools. These include the tools in Adobe's Creative Suite (especially Photoshop and InDesign), as well as Adobe Reader, Microsoft PowerPoint and Word, and video-editing suites, such as Adobe Premier and Avid's Interplay. Most provide players for various audio and video formats, including Adobe Flash, Apple QuickTime, and Microsoft Windows Media. A move is taking place to drop support of older file types, and most modern-day DAM systems use HTML5-embedded codes to deliver the video directly from the DAM or content distribution network (CDN) into websites and other touchpoints across the content journey.

Close integration allows you to search, access, and save assets across both the system and the tool, and presents these actions well within the context of the tool. A high degree of transparency in performing operations enhances your experience and allows you to focus on the task and not how the tool is connected to the DAM.

Some vendors, such as OpenText and EMC, have also made significant efforts to allow you to work with files in the file system. You can easily drag and drop them for ingestion into the DAM. This makes loading of assets much easier. DAM systems vary in how they allow you to attach metadata to the assets you ingest in this manner, however.

Ultimately, though, usability means "fitness to purpose." Therefore, you cannot understand ease of use outside the context of business process. It also means that an enterprise that cares about meaningful and broad adoption of its DAM system will likely have to invest in modifying default user interfaces for different roles, tasks, or scenarios. You should have a clear idea of how to do that in the DAM systems you consider and how much effort it will require.

A Special Note About Standards

Vendors love to talk about standards. To be sure, standards are important, but there are fewer standards than you would think. Moreover, even those are less standardized than we'd like. Keep in mind that whichever boxes the vendors check, standards support tends to be a relative attribute rather than an absolute. There are different ways to comply with J2EE or to support the Dublin Core specification. You need to focus on how a particular tool supports a particular standard. In the following sections, we outline some standards that you might want to explore before you begin—or re-embark on—your DAM journey.

Currently, there are no definitive standards within the digital asset management industry. We see some standards as they relate to certain metadata standards (XMP, Dublin Core, and IPTC as outlined next). As the chaos continues in enterprise-based workflows, the need for an interoperability standard is clear.

Dublin Core

The Dublin Core metadata element set is a standard for interoperable, cross-domain information resource description. It provides a simple and standard set of conventions for describing items, making them easier to find, and enabling more intelligent information discovery systems. Dublin Core is widely used to describe digital materials such as video, sound, image, text, and web pages. Because of its simplicity, all DAM systems support Dublin Core in some form. There is, however, no body for qualifying, testing, or approving the implementation.

When you're a DAM system buyer and user, this lack of an absolute standard can be critical, because Dublin Core provides a basic set of metadata fields that may be implemented differently in different DAM systems. As a result, while it may be likely that one system using Dublin Core can exchange information with another system using it, you cannot be certain. If you're relying on Dublin Core as a key part of your metadata model, be sure to understand how the vendor implements it.

"Dublin" refers to Dublin, Ohio, where the Online Computer Library Center (OCLC) originated the work in 1995. "Core" refers to the fact that the metadata element set is a basic but expandable "core" list. The semantics of Dublin Core were established and are maintained by an international, cross-disciplinary group of professionals from library science, computer science, text encoding, museums, and other related fields. The Dublin Core Metadata Initiative (DCMI) maintains and evolves the standard.

This standard has two levels: simple and qualified. Simple Dublin Core includes 15 metadata elements:

- Title
- Creator
- Subject
- Description
- Publisher
- Contributor
- Date
- Type
- Format
- Identifier
- Source
- Language
- Relation
- Coverage
- Rights

Each Dublin Core element is optional and may be repeated. Dublin Core has no prescribed order for presenting or using the elements.

Qualified Dublin Core adds three additional elements—Audience, Provenance, and Rights Holder—as well as a group of elements that refine the semantics in ways that may be useful in resource discovery. Qualified Dublin Core also includes a set of recommended encoding schemes that are designed to aid in the interpretation of an element value. These schemes include controlled vocabularies and formal notations or parsing rules.

Historically, many DAM implementations have started with Dublin Core. We're not sure why. Perhaps users wanted a well-defined starter set of metadata for describing assets. In some situations, such as with museums, Dublin Core was a common element in the museum information model. Therefore, if you don't have an information model or a taxonomy for your assets, Dublin Core may provide you with a very basic starting point. However, we have found that most implementations quickly outgrow this core or expand it so significantly for their particular use case or domain that it becomes barely recognizable.

Dublin Core does not appear to be frequently used for asset transfer or interoperability. XML and XMP allow for easier mappings between systems using XSLT, for example, to transform tags from one system to another. Thus, the Dublin Core—or any metadata model for that matter—would be expressed into XML or XMP for output. It would then be mapped back into another system's metadata model, according to a set of proprietary syntactic and semantic rules.

IPTC

A group of news organizations established the International Press Telecommunications Council (IPTC) in 1965 to safeguard the telecommunications interests of the world's press. Based in the UK, the council is a consortium of the world's major news agencies, publishers, and industry vendors. Virtually every major news organization in the world uses the IPTC's technical standards for improved news exchange.

Since the late 1970s, the IPTC has focused on developing and publishing industry standards for the interchange of news data. In particular, the IPTC defined a set of metadata attributes to apply to images. Although the IPTC defined the standards in 1979, the concept advanced significantly in 1994 when Adobe created a specification for actually embedding the metadata into digital image files. These "IPTC headers" can be embedded into JPEG, EXIF, or TIFF formatted image files.

Photographers and printers commonly use IPTC metadata to store information about the digital images directly in the files. Applications, such as a DAM system, can read and write this information, facilitating workflows and communicating additional or needed information. Most DAMs support IPTC—particularly its extraction from the image file. Some systems support write-back, which inserts the metadata back into the file.

XMP

Adobe developed the Extensible Metadata Platform (XMP) in 2001. It is an XML schema for the same metadata as IPTC, but is based on XML/RDF (Resource Description Framework), a general-purpose language for representing information on the Web. It is inherently extensible. Adobe and the IPTC collaborated to produce the IPTC Core Schema for XMP, which merges the two approaches to embedded metadata. The XMP specification describes techniques for embedding the metadata in a variety of files including JPEG, TIFF, JPEG 2000, GIF, PNG, HTML, PostScript, PDF, SVG, Adobe Illustrator, and DNG files. Recent versions of Adobe's Creative Suite products—Photoshop, Illustrator, and Bridge—support XMP, as do a small but increasing number of third-party tools.

Adobe, the XMP Open group, and some DAM vendors assert that an asset's metadata should be embedded in the file and carried with it wherever it goes outside the DAM system. Historically, metadata in the DAM system remained separate from the asset. The DAM system didn't typically attach or reinsert the metadata into the file once it left the system. With the XMP approach, the DAM system (as well as other systems) can process it more intelligently and make more intelligent use of the asset.

Systems embracing the XMP approach can at least perform XMP metadata extraction. They can read the file's XMP information and use those definitions and structures to map the values from the file into metadata fields in the DAM. Some systems go further and use this information to guide the creation of new metadata schemas, such as definitions of metadata types and metadata fields, in the DAM system. This is a step beyond metadata extraction. It creates new DAM schema on the fly so that it can represent what XMP contains in the file. This capability can provide additional system versatility. You would potentially be able to dynamically create or modify the metadata model on the fly, using XMP, without system downtime.

This perspective is pushing an emerging trend: XMP-based workflows, systems, tools, and processes that are informed by and (in some cases) driven by the asset's embedded XMP information. Thus, XMP will be useful to you if you expect to create more automated workflows or if you expect your files to have embedded metadata. We see this use of XMP particularly in advertising, prepress, and print use cases.

From a technical standpoint, transformation engines primarily handle the process of inserting and extracting XMP into and out of files. They perform this function at asset import or export, or sometimes as part of transforming an asset, so it can affect ingest, export, or transformation performance. It may, however, be buried in the overall ingest or transformation performance, so it may not be easily identifiable as a performance problem area. Metadata inserted into a file can increase the asset size, although for high-resolution images, this increase may be dwarfed by the size of the image itself.

Injecting metadata into an asset can change an asset from a binary comparison perspective. This is critical because many DAM systems use algorithms that examine the asset at a binary level to determine whether it is unique or already exists in the DAM system. Injecting metadata into the asset can change the outcome of this "checksum" algorithm, and thus create duplicate assets in the DAM. While you might argue that the asset hasn't changed, its metadata has.

Some file formats don't currently support XMP. When working with assets in one of these file formats, you need to use another approach, such as "side cars" and related files. In these approaches, the XMP information lives near or is appended to the file. Some vendors support this approach. Be aware that this approach can affect ingest and export and may not itself be supported for all file formats. You may encounter a problem if you want to have full XMP workflows using assets with XMP embedded metadata.

If you're considering XMP, ask the vendor what happens in this case and whether the extraction of the metadata occurs before the system performs checksum or uniqueness calculation on the asset. Additionally, ask about the performance and asset size increases to get a sense of whether this would be a significant factor. In most cases, you will not encounter a significant performance problem.

Web Services Versus REST

Web services refers to a related set of protocols and technologies designed to enable applications to expose discrete features to each other over the Internet. Instead of hypertext, think of hyperservices. Much of the fervor around Web services has centered on marketplace integration and bundling B2C and B2B applications into a single transaction. Nevertheless, there is still a major DAM story, but much of it will happen within and as part of the enterprise network.

Web services stands on three interrelated standards:

- **SOAP:** The transport protocol that enables disparate applications to plug into each other seamlessly as services

- **WSDL:** The language for describing those services

- **UDDI:** The directory protocol for listing those services

Each of these standards uses XML.

REST stands for Representational State Transfer. It is another approach to providing and consuming discrete services using Internet protocols. With REST, services are mapped to URLs, and you serve or invoke any function through a GET, PUT, or POST to a URL. A REST-based DAM system enables you to invoke any standard operation in a repository through a URL and to access alternate versions or kick off a workflow by adding additional parameters to the POST or GET request.

DAM system managers recognize several benefits from a more service-oriented approach:

- **Connecting better from desktop editing tools to back-end DAMs:** Facilitating the transparent movement of assets between the desktop application and the DAM system and vice versa is a key element of successfully adopting a DAM system and streamlining workflow processes. While some approaches rely on native interfaces at the file system level to perform this function, Web services allow your creative and Office applications to search for, access, and save assets and then use them directly and seamlessly with the DAM system. Some vendors already use Web services to connect the DAM system to authoring tools and other applications.

- **Integrating content silos, improving brand consistency, and removing redundancy and cost:** Enterprises need interenterprise workflow today. The core problems are a lack of standards and silos of creativity and storage. Note, however, that we could often say the same thing of interdepartmental workflows within large, decentralized enterprises. I've seen brand marketing teams or corporate marketing teams within the same enterprise perform similar creative activities yet regenerate content because they can't locate it, they can't share it, or they don't even know about it! You'll see this occur with PowerPoint slides, even in small organizations, with everyone keeping and modifying copies on their desktop but no one controlling or owning the master or "released" version. The same problem happens with assets like logos, images, common charts and graphics, and other brand elements. A more SOA-oriented model enables the enterprise to offer central DAM services and desktop editing tool access for regional, local branches of the enterprise that still need to localize content or generate their own marketing collateral.

- **Creating an "enterprise service bus" for rich media:** DAM integration historically followed the same path as enterprise application integration (EAI)—point-to-point solutions. In contrast, an SOA-oriented approach would expose generic DAM services to other applications that can utilize their logic with the DAM system. Media and entertainment companies have taken the lead in this area. They have created enterprise service bus-based infrastructures built on SOA to facilitate the development of a range of applications that integrate a variety of other services and applications. In an SOA world, it shouldn't matter which tool or applications you license; they interoperate via SOAP or REST.

JSR 170/JSR 283/JCR

JSR 170 (now JSR 283)—sometimes known as *Java Content Repository*, or JCR—is a specification developed under the Java Community Process (JCP) program. This expert group contains more than 60 individual members representing both major content management vendors and Java technology infrastructure players like Apache, IBM, and Oracle.

The goal is to provide greater code portability above the repository layer. Today, nearly all content management applications, including DAM systems, ship with their own "content repository" (usually proprietary). This repository usually extends a storage layer, such as a relational database, with the various service facilities that almost any modern content application requires. Nearly every vendor implements its "repository services" differently, using different terminologies and programming interfaces.

To the Java world (and possibly beyond), JCR promises a unified API that allows accessing any compliant repository in a vendor or implementation-neutral fashion. This would lead to the separation of concerns that characterize modern IT architectures. Some people call JCR the "JDBC of Content Repositories."

The JSR 170/283 specification defines how an application and a content repository interact with respect to a number of content services. For example, the versioning facilities of a content repository are clearly defined, so an application knows how to browse the version history, check in and check out content items, or update and merge content in a standard fashion.

JCR compliance has different levels. While some DAM vendors have implemented JCR, few (other than Adobe) support it at all levels. If your enterprise already leverages JCR heavily in an existing enterprise content management system, there's a chance you may be able to realize some efficiencies by choosing a DAM system that implements JCR and that (as a result) can integrate relatively smoothly with the ECM system. Otherwise, JCR is probably not something that should be determinative in your choice of DAM system.

CHAPTER 8

Cloud, On-Premise, or Hybrid? DAM Delivery Models

When you buy DAM software, several possible deployment model options are available. Although DAM systems have been on-premise traditionally, cloud-based options have proliferated. When we say "cloud-based," we mean to what extent a particular solution can be deployed in a cloud, by you, the DAM vendor, or a third party. While this solution is often portrayed as "just put it in the cloud," it's not quite that simple in practice.

As enterprises seek to decrease infrastructure spending and free up IT resources, the cloud has risen to the forefront on many agendas. Cloud deployments offer several advantages, such as ease of virtualization, elasticity, resource pooling, and scalability.

Cloud definitions vary, and there are many types of cloud services. You need to distinguish among private cloud, public cloud, SaaS, and hybrid models. The important point here is that all cloud models obviate the need to run DAM technology on-premise.

When vendors say they "do cloud," this expression could mean a variety of things, which are outlined next. Then, for each vendor, we show whether it offers the following options.

Option 1: On-Premise

In the first scenario, you manage the software, usually in your own corporate environment, hence, "on-premise." In what's called a "managed hosting" environment, the hardware can be self-managed or managed by a third party. You own the environment, and there are no cloud characteristics or advantages such as virtualization—unless you set that up yourself.

In a third-party, managed hosting scenario, the vendor (or one of its partners) offers managed hosting on a traditional version of the software in a data center somewhere. You still have control over customizing, extending, and upgrading the software; the vendor is just replacing your hardware and network connections with its own.

One key consideration here—and a potential disadvantage of on-premise software—is whether the software is virtualizable, and if so, whether it has been certified with different VM platforms. Some on-premise data centers deal with application elasticity by employing virtualization services, an inherent feature of cloud deployment models.

Option 2: Private Cloud

Private cloud is similar to on-premise, in that you still manage the DAM software itself, and it lives behind some sort of enterprise firewall. Now, though, it runs atop a cloud platform that can bring typical cloud benefits such as virtualization, elasticity, resource pooling, and so on.

Therefore, you should examine some of the same architectural considerations of public clouds, particularly around whether the DAM software is certified to run in your particular flavor of private cloud stack.

Private cloud-based implementations require the same—or an even higher—level of skills and resources as are required for an on-premise installation.

Option 3: Public Cloud

In the third scenario, you put your DAM in a public cloud service, such as Rackspace, Amazon, or Microsoft Azure. You'll find many variants here. You could host your DAM on-premise but take advantage of cloud elasticity for your asset delivery and transformation/transcoding infrastructure to support global delivery or spikes in traffic and file processing. Alternatively, you could host your DAM application in the cloud and keep your assets on-premise.

Note that the DAM vendor (or its partners) may or may not manage your relationship with the cloud provider.

In addition, the DAM vendor may or may not convert its one-time license fee into a monthly subscription model. As always, you will need to pay more money to the cloud vendor to achieve greater levels of redundancy, reliability, and global dispersion. Also, don't forget the cost and hassle of virtual private network connections to your cloud instances.

As with the previous two options, you are still running "traditional software" as a dedicated instance, and you are responsible for whatever changes you make to the application, unless the vendor includes that as a managed service. Note that not all on-premise solutions work in the cloud today, and many that do have been certified with only one cloud vendor.

Option 4: Software as a Service

In the fourth approach, vendors have built a multitenant, SaaS solution from the ground up. Note that these solutions didn't historically run in a public cloud but were hosted in the vendor's own (redundant) infrastructures. Vendors are now offering alternative public cloud options such as Amazon, Google, and Microsoft Azure. However, even if they run their own hosting environment, they have the benefit of elasticity and monthly billing for hosting and the DAM application itself, with no initial license fees (however, you typically need to pay a setup fee).

Many of these vendors also serve as your "integrator," and perhaps even agency, since they know their platform best and typically don't have many partnerships outside development firms. They also take care of upgrades, which tend to come in frequent, albeit small bursts. Some customers are surprised to discover that they typically don't have a choice of whether—or when—to upgrade.

Option 5: Hybrid

Hybrid installations are, as the name implies, a mixture of cloud and on-premise models, which can include any combination of one or more of the preceding approaches. You may want to have your software hosted and maintained by a third party; however, you may decide not to do this with your assets and data for security reasons. In a hybrid model, you can maintain physical control over your assets and data while using a cloud-based platform, in some cases approaching the maintenance and support features that pure SaaS brings to the table.

One popular use of the hybrid model is called cloud "bursting." In this case, you use the cloud only for elasticity when you have spikes in activity or data. In bandwidth-intensive environments and when heavy archival needs are present, hybrid models are appropriate in DAM.

Many vendors now offer you the ability to "point" to on-site servers to access assets or back up data stored in the DAM system to a physical location (or multiple locations) that you denote. This combination of features from on-premise and cloud-delivery models goes some way to appease detractors who worry about throwing all their data into the cloud. Hybrid has had a slow uptake in the DAM industry, but we're expecting provisions to increase in the space.

Table 8.1 summarizes all these features.

Remember, be wary of hosting companies and other vendor partners that take on-premise software and convert it to multitenancy to sell as a shared service to more customers. This approach frequently does not end well, since software designed for a single customer often does not have the right security mechanisms in place to run for multiple customers off just one instance.

Now let's turn to some more general cloud considerations. In every case shown in Table 8.1, you need to address special issues and ensure that you have some key elements in place:

- Sufficient and secure network connections to your remote instances.

- Trust in the vendor's security model and procedures. The vendor knows this and usually has strong controls in place, but you still should check.

- An awareness of the potential for outages or disruptions caused by other customers.

- An understanding of who is going to perform backups and where.

- A clear outline of who is responsible for each layer in the stack, including the following:

  - Network

  - Hardware

  - Operating system

  - Application server

  - Data

  - DAM applications: management and delivery

  - Caching and/or CDN

- A clear plan for handling authentication and authorization, including integration with on-premise identity management and SSO systems.

- Knowledge for how you will integrate with other enterprise systems if necessary.

- A plan for migrating your content out of the cloud in a non-proprietary format for you to use elsewhere if you change your provider.

TABLE 8.1 CLOUD DEPLOYMENT OPTIONS

	On-Premise	Private Cloud
Software/Hardware Management	You or third party	You or third party
Software/Hardware Ownership	You	You or third party
Cloud properties	No. In an on-premise environment, you have to worry only about your internal network configuration. In cloud environments, you have to worry about your bandwidth pipes/traffic into and from the cloud providers.	Virtualization, resource pooling, elasticity, and scalability.
Analogy	Buying wine, storing, and drinking it in your own house; maybe you have a house/cellar manager.	Buying wine, storing, and drinking it in your own house; maybe you have a house manager, but you own it. The manager can create more space in the house if you acquire a lot more wine or have more people drinking, especially simultaneously.

Here's the bottom line: vendors, consultants, and analysts throw around the term *cloud* loosely. Be sure you understand exactly what you're getting when you sign the contract. The decision lines here are usually drawn by IT, based on their comfort levels.

Storage and Archiving

Storage management refers to the storage, retrieval, management, and eventual archiving of files and metadata. Every DAM must somehow manage where assets live, how metadata is stored, and the breadth of storage types that can be used with the system over the lifetime of the asset. Depending on the scope and scale of your deployment, storage management could be an important consideration. If you choose a SaaS or cloud system, you will not be

Public Cloud	SaaS	Hybrid
Third party	Third party	You and/or third party
Third party	Third party	You and/or third party
Same as private cloud, plus options for infrastructure as a service (hardware, servers, switches, and so on), platform as a service (infra + database, developer services, and so on); Opex rather than Capex for services.	Full equation of infrastructure + platform + application.	Any combination of options from private and public cloud.
Buying and having wine at a public wine bar.	Monthly contract with bar/restaurant that allows you to use its premises and offers you wine as part of the contract.	N/A.

as concerned with storage management. If you plan to install the software on premise, your IT group and the administrator will need to consider storage management.

Storage management includes

- The underlying mechanisms for storing, retrieving, and managing assets—files and metadata. Examples include database, files system, and raw disk partitions.

- The integration and management of external stores and storage types, such as spinning disk, near line, off-line, archival, tape libraries, storage area networks (SANs), network attached storage (NAS), and RAID arrays.

- The transition from one type of storage to another or one state to another. Examples include transitioning from live to archived or archived to live.

DAM Storage

Storage costs seem to be dropping each year, but given the vast quantities of audio and video media companies are dealing with, storage is a big-ticket item for broadcasters, and they strive to achieve an optimal balance between storage cost and performance. Following are the different types of storage media companies may use:

- **Broadcast storage:** A video server stores high-quality media files intended for immediate playout. These servers are meant for high performance and are specifically built for broadcast purposes; not surprisingly, broadcast storage is the most expensive among the different storage alternatives.

- **Online storage:** In this option, frequently used files or files that were just ingested are stored. These files are used in the content production process and multiple users access them. Examples of online storage solutions include NAS, SANs, and high-end disk array systems optimized for fast read-writes.

- **Near online storage:** Also called *near-line storage*, this type holds occasionally used videos (such as IDE disk drives). Disk access speeds are slower than online storage. These videos are meant to be accessed by a limited number of users, but this option is less expensive than online storage.

- **Offline or archival storage:** This option houses infrequently accessed media files and programs that were broadcast and are maintained as archives. Examples of solutions include robot-arm-operated tape libraries and CD (or DVD) jukeboxes. This is the cheapest form of storage, but it also has slower access and retrieval.

For broadcasters, storage management entails balancing cost, frequency of use, and accessibility. A storage policy determines which media files should reside on what type of storage, and how and under what circumstances they should be transferred to the various storage options. As you can imagine, a storage policy could range from simple with a few basic rules to very complex, involving multiple different sites and rules.

DAM systems can be used to handle simple storage policies and provide necessary file management functionality. However, when complex storage policy implementation is required, it is usually done with a combination of DAM and a hierarchical storage management (HSM) system. When DAM is integrated with an HSM solution, the HSM handles file movements and retrieval in the context of the broadcast workflow.

On the surface, storage management appears largely concerned with what physical storage a DAM system can support and the physical storage location and type of storage for each asset's file. It also deals with the system's capabilities to manage, monitor, and handle problems when accessing and moving assets among various storage types, and with the logical view of an asset, which means hiding its underlying physical location to the end user while making it easy for an administrator to manage. For example, if you are using SAN or NAS storage, you need to determine if the asset management system can handle it and how transparently.

Database Storage

Most systems use a database to store metadata and a managed file system to store the asset's files. Systems typically support Oracle, Microsoft SQL Server, an open source database such as MySQL, or in rare instances IBM DB2. Be sure to check that the vendor supports your flavor of database.

The asset management system supports a file store, which is typically (but not always) a managed file system. It takes over either a raw disk partition or some section of the file system in which to manage assets. It should provide a range of capabilities for monitoring the capacity, use, and utilization of the file store. Additionally, it should be able to allocate new file stores, determine when to migrate, and balance between clustered storage.

Distributed File Stores

Some systems support distributed file stores. For example, some assets live in New York, whereas others live in Los Angeles and the archive is in Des Moines. The system manages references to remotely stored assets. If the system doesn't directly manage the asset, such as a very large video that lives in a remote SAN, it does its best to maintain access and resolve access problems. Key issues in distributed storage have to do with asset accessibility and movement. The goal is to minimize the movement of the actual file, using proxies whenever possible. You should move the file only when absolutely necessary, such as with video workflows. Many of the storage vendors that provide technology to the broadcast and film industry have specialized storage systems that integrate well with asset management systems.

Archives

Enterprise DAM systems generally need deeper support for storage management. They typically integrate with and support a variety of storage types and are more fluid in moving media among them. An administrative console controls movement and changes of state. These systems also may provide some degree of automation and scheduling. Systems vary in their support for archiving, integrating with, or handling a variety of storage types. Some organizations have very specific needs for "deep archiving," which certain vendors support; be sure to ask about this capability if it is important to you.

Cold Storage

In what could be considered a manifestation of the ideas behind hybrid implementations, we see the DAM community beginning to adopt cold storage as an archive option, allowing for cheap mass storage of assets and data that are no longer in active use. AWS Glacier is the most commonly used medium for cold storage, which is being used to store terabytes of inactive data for a number of DAM vendors. Buyer beware: This is only a cheap option if data remains "cold," and should not be considered for archives that are frequently accessed to reactivate old content. If you want a cheap and simple way to push a large amount of data somewhere for "safe keeping," cold storage might be part of your strategy.

CHAPTER 9

You're Not Just Buying a Tool: Strategic Considerations

The DAM market consists of global, regional, and local vendors (see Figure 9.1). Strategic considerations can vary considerably among vendors depending on their provenance, size, and other factors. The fit of a particular vendor to your enterprise needs, culture, and orientation is as critical to your overall success as the suitability of its DAM product. In the following sections, we describe what other factors to consider when looking at any product.

FIGURE 9.1
The vendor ecosystem.

Vendor Professional Services

In the typical DAM project, customers spend more on services than on software, sometimes two to five times more. To meet customers' consulting needs, most vendors maintain their own professional services organization (PSO). Most vendors also have a "partner channel" around their products, with which they may even compete. These integrators, partners, and resellers can help implement the package. The ability of partner channels varies dramatically from vendor to vendor and can change over time

When possible, you should find experienced services geographically close to you to avoid paying for consultants' hefty travel costs.

Investigate a potential partner's "soft" skills, such as information architecture and a good sensitivity to organizational issues, in addition to product knowledge. Doubly investigate a partner's product knowledge because some partnerships are in name only and integrator skill and expertise can fluctuate wildly from product to product—even from the same vendor. Perform as careful diligence of all consultancies as you did of the product itself.

Don't overlook the possibility of bringing in an independent developer or consultant to provide knowledge and assistance. Products with longevity in the market typically boast more—and more experienced—consultants. Many of these consultants are alumni of vendor PSOs, which tend to have high staff turnover. On the other hand, the longer a tool has been out there, the higher the demand for these independent consultants, so the more they cost. Always require documentation for independent work done on your system.

Like support, many factors influence the quality of the implementation services you receive. Vendors often have "A" teams of their top-notch implementation consultants—and then everyone else. "A" teams tend to work only on the biggest or most prominent client projects. "Everybody else" within a vendor PSO can include contractors that the vendor may or may not have trained on its tool.

The vendor's own PSO knows the product best but may be stuck in older ways of doing things. The PSO may not be up to speed on—or even favor—the product's latest capabilities and modules. It may also bring a set of informal, subsidiary modules to your implementation that the company does not officially support as part of your separate software license agreement. Be sure to understand any potential exposures here.

For open source platforms, the availability and quality of services matters even more, because many of them tend to be complex to install and configure. As in the commercial world, tension builds between the project "founders" and other firms trying to make money providing services and support. You may end up working with a mixed team of core project founders and local developers, much as you might with a commercial vendor. This places a premium on your ability to manage multisupplier projects.

SaaS vendors tend to provide an array of services. That's how they make money, and the major SaaS/cloud players are generally good at it. The downside is that they typically don't have strong partner channels because they tend to do most of the services work themselves. Therefore, you may need to get comfortable working with an off-site consulting team when you sign on with a SaaS provider.

In almost all cases, selecting a "hot" vendor or product has a big downside. Consultants who know the tool will be in high demand. As a result, they will likely be scarce, expensive, and itinerant. Without adequate expertise, you may lose the added advantage that the innovative technology was supposed to bring. Before you select a tool, make sure you know where, when, and how you are going to line up the necessary expertise to implement it properly.

Integration and Partnerships

How effectively does the vendor's technology mesh with that from other suppliers? First, let's note that not all integrations include a formal partnership. Second, a partnership doesn't guarantee effective integration between two vendors' products because most vendors enter into partnerships for business and sales purposes, not to accomplish a firm technical objective.

Caveats aside, some vendors seem innately more open to integration with complementary or adjacent technologies. They don't necessarily have more open APIs; rather, they make a point of being more conducive to integration. Other vendors have a culture of trying to build everything themselves.

The depth of a specific integration to another tool that is very important to your enterprise may matter more than the breadth of a vendor's partnerships. If, for example, your enterprise uses SAP for billing and accounting, the ability to integrate seamlessly to that environment to exchange metadata may become paramount. Some DAM vendors pay close attention to their relationships with Microsoft to the exclusion of nearly all other third-party suppliers, giving them tight integrations with the latest server and client technology from Redmond. The only way to know if a partnership or integration is real is to talk to customers who have put the two technologies together in a production environment. Ask detailed questions about the level of effort and methodologies required. Don't be surprised if they need substantial professional services.

Most DAM vendors have put their energies around Web services in general—and SOAP in particular—regardless of the performance and security shortcomings that still exist with that model. A more REST-oriented approach borders on nonexistent. Don't expect to be able to easily remove discrete services from or insert them into your DAM Web services.

Channel Professional Services: Support and Community

All technology buyers want to know, "How well does the vendor support the product?" All vendors rave about their product support. Nearly all customers complain about vendor support. What's going on here?

Factors Affecting Support

Many factors determine whether a vendor's support will meet your needs. One key consideration is that vendors often offer different support mechanisms in different countries or locales. These differences may include different hours of support or varying expectations about how much first- and second-line support will be handled by a local partner. In general, the larger the vendor, the more variable you'll find first-line support. Some large vendors outsource it. That's not necessarily a bad thing, but the person on the other line may never have actually performed an implementation of the product. Many small companies let customers reach "real" engineers in times of acute trouble. Smaller vendors, however, often have difficulty providing the 24/7 support that enterprise customers have come to expect. In almost all cases, you can elect to spend more for higher levels of support.

It is a fact of the software business that a vendor's larger and more prominent customers receive better support. Agreeing to take reference calls and speaking at user conferences also doesn't hurt. Of course, you don't necessarily want to be a vendor's biggest customer if it doesn't have the capacity to support you adequately.

Rest assured that the day will come when you will need to escalate a problem up through or beyond your vendor's support department. If you are a small fish in that vendor's pond, your chances of getting what you want drop substantially compared to your larger brethren. Customers who have contracted with their vendor's professional services organization sometimes later turn informally to the specialists who worked with them when a problem crops up, but don't count on it.

In general, cloud-centric software-as-a-service vendors provide better support because they're on the hook for monthly fees from you. They are also more likely to support your designated lead users as well as your developers. Traditional vendors typically ask you to support your contributors while they support the software. In addition, SaaS vendors are providing a service, so the line between professional consulting and support becomes a bit blurrier. To that end, be sure that your support contract with a SaaS provider clearly defines what constitutes tech support and what constitutes site enhancements.

Regardless of whether you end up with SaaS or you acquire the software, it's a best practice to funnel all support calls to a central log within your company—even if multiple people are calling support. This helps you understand if there are systemic software defects—or perhaps see the need for better training. It will also greatly help with your vendor relationships if you have good insight into the patterns of your calls, especially when something needs to be escalated.

Community Strength

A thriving DAM community has formed across all asset management users. Thriving user communities provide informal support in the form of peer interactions and user group meetings. Alas, your support needs will have to be met by the vendor and its partner ecosystem. Within this environment, does the vendor provide you with access to other users of its product? A small but growing factor is the availability of authentic community support, including vendor developers, integrators, and customers. Few commercial vendors have attempted to match the level of support ecosystem that you can find in an open source software community. Don't underestimate the value of this kind of informal support. Vendor user-group meetings are also extremely helpful, allowing direct interactions with your peers. These group meetings also give larger or more geographically focused vendors additional leverage to compensate for their own somewhat impersonal support channels. Developer extranets are rare but invaluable. We encourage you to take advantage of meetups if you live in London, New York City, Chicago, Los Angeles, or Washington, DC. You also may benefit from the Henry Stewart DAM conferences and the DAM Foundation.

Documentation

You should not rely solely on a vendor's documentation to teach, explain, or even adequately document how a system works. Instead, invest in formal training for both developers and contributors; also, cultivate relationships with the vendor's developers and other product licensees in your industry.

Maintenance

Your support contract with your vendor typically includes "maintenance." Examine the language very carefully to be sure what it covers. It often covers free software upgrades and patches, but the devil is in the details. Sometimes vendors declare that a new major version of a product, usually after a major platform overhaul or change, actually constitutes a completely new product. Therefore, you have to pay a fee for the pleasure of upgrading or, in this case, replacing existing software. Vendors frequently release add-on modules at additional cost. Sometimes, these modules are snippets of code or subsystems that were part of the main product but are now marketed separately. Traditional vendor business practice holds that the best way to grow is to obtain new revenues from existing customers. Closely examine your maintenance contracts accordingly.

Remember also that while maintenance covers the actual software patches and releases, it almost never covers the labor involved in migrating to the newer version. Be sure to budget for these services. Depending on the scale and complexity of your implementation, this process can take days, weeks, or even months to accomplish. SaaS vendors tend to have a leg up in this area. Because they tightly control the environment, they can easily upgrade customers, often without their even knowing it.

Strategy and Roadmap

Some vendors have a clearer and more passionate sense for what the market wants and orient their product development accordingly. Others develop software in more of a vacuum and then see what sticks.

We value clarity of vision and strategy more than expansiveness. A vendor obsessed with becoming a winner across multiple scenarios probably won't satisfy any single customer very well. Therefore, we look for focus. Does the vendor have a clear idea of which use cases fit best for its product? Has it structured its development accordingly? You should look for this, too, but remember that vendor-marketing messages tend to blur distinctions and create a false sense of omnipotence among vendor salespeople.

Be sure that your vendor truly understands asset management with respect to the following issues:

- DAM-oriented information architecture

- Workflow and feature needs for creative and marketing teams

- Domain-specific knowledge (for example, print, video, broadcast, and production)

- DAM application development

- Application technology and service trends on the Web

As contradictory as it sounds, don't assume that a digital asset management vendor truly understands digital asset management. In fact, many suppliers, especially large vendors who sell other "enterprise" content management, have a very limited and dated vision of what contemporary enterprises want to accomplish with a DAM system. Furthermore, given the breadth of application of DAM systems, a given vendor may have little experience in your specific scenario or use case.

Viability and Stability

If strategy is one side of the vendor's organizational coin, then execution is the other. Buyers tell us that they want stability and predictability from their software suppliers. In a fast-moving marketplace, that can be hard to find. We consider stability in very broad terms, across three general categories: product, product changes, and financial viability and M&A activity (see Figure 9.2).

- How stable is the product or service in production? Does it hiccup regularly? Where? Why? All software is buggy, but some software is worse than others. More importantly, some vendors have a habit of regularly releasing under-tested code into production.

  Are changes underway or planned? Migrations frequently become painful for customers. We are generally leery of products that are about to receive a major technology refresh. The last thing you want to do after spending half a year or more on a DAM implementation is to go through a major upgrade or wholesale replacement. Of course, recently upgraded products are not always ideal candidates either. Vendors may think that they understand new platforms and technologies, but they often do not—particularly when it comes to performance. This doesn't mean you should avoid products that have been newly re-architected, but you should go in with your eyes open. It's always a thoughtful reference-call question to ask about the upgrade experience, and at the same time, ask the vendor about account attrition and retention. This is not to encourage a "rush to judg-ment"; every vendor has some long-term and some lost clients. Your value here is knowing the why behind these experiences.

- Is the vendor financially viable, and are there potential merg-ers and acquisitions (M&A), disruptions, and opportunities? While this examination is necessarily subjective, there are clear markers, including cash position, sales trends, and whether acquisitions constitute a good fit. M&A activity isn't as rampart as in previous years, but it does happen—as does strategic realignment and reprioritizing within the larger vendors. Be sure to research these facts for yourself.

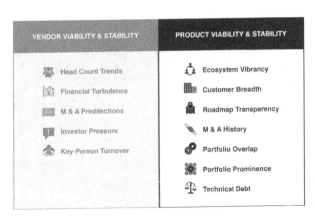

FIGURE 9.2
Vendor and product viability and stability.

CHAPTER 10

Universal Scenarios: The Key to Comparing Technologies

The right solution for you is the one that *meets your needs*, not necessarily one that an ivory-tower analyst who has never touched a DAM put in the top right corner of a not-so-magic quadrant. Scenario analysis is an efficient approach to understanding your needs.

While not always by vendor design, DAM products are better—and worse—fits for different use cases. There is no one product that is a great fit for every scenario. The 14 common scenarios described in this chapter, combined with an understanding of the strengths and weaknesses of any product you are considering, will help you identify which products could be a good fit for you.

These scenarios are abstractions and the use cases overlap. In practice, your own digital asset management effort will most likely be a combination of scenarios. Nonetheless, scenarios help you understand which types of products tend to work for which types of projects and situations.

These scenarios also give you a framework for developing your own unique set of scenarios. Scenarios make it easier to communicate your needs within your organization, as well as with vendors, systems integrators, and consultants. It's an interesting exercise to revisit your scenarios at set points after implementation and go live. You may find that you have met some, changed several, dropped a couple, and maybe forgotten one. Properly used, scenarios offer a great discussion point with upper management and can help guide approvals and provide a framework for ongoing budgeting conversations.

These scenarios for implementing a DAM system revolve around different types of digital asset applications and workflows. We break them down into four broad categories, although some scenarios could be placed into multiple categories. In trying to match your own needs, focus less on the category and more on the individual scenarios. The core scenarios are as follows:

Image and Brand Management

- Scenario 1: DAM library or photo archive
- Scenario 2: Brand-centric asset management
- Scenario 3: Multilingual brand management
- Scenario 4: Advertising and marketing asset management

- Scenario 5: Periodical and catalog production and management
- Scenario 6: Multichannel publishing

Corporate Time-Based Media Management

- Scenario 7: Audio and video library review and approval
- Scenario 8: Audio and video production and reuse

Broadcast Media Management

- Scenario 9: Television news
- Scenario 10: Sports broadcasting
- Scenario 11: Feature-length TV and cinema
- Scenario 12: Radio broadcasting
- Scenario 13: Media modernization and archives
- Scenario 14: Parliaments, government, military, and judicial

Image and Brand Management

These scenarios are the most basic, and they get more complex as you move down the list. Image and brand management scenarios focus uniquely on managing brand assets and images, with little to no video management needs.

Scenario 1: DAM Library or Photo Archive

A common starting point and basic use of a DAM system is as a digital asset library or photo archive. Your DAM system functions as a common, centralized place to catalog and store all of your digital photos or assorted assets. These assets may be at the end of a creative process, older, or used infrequently. For example, the archive becomes a reference for the following:

- Historical use of the assets.
- Generation of new ideas, such as using an old picture in a new brochure.
- Scene re-creation, such as seeing what the set for a photo shoot looked like.

- A "reference library," such as images of taillight and headlight designs from 100 years of automotive manufacturing—acting as a rich source of insight and ideas for design work.

In essence, these scenarios set forth the idea of a single, definitive catalog to determine what the organization owns. It requires only core DAM capabilities, including a basic information model and metadata support, simple asset rendition support, a relatively simple security model, strong search/browse/navigation, and the ability to view and download assets.

This type of DAM system works for museums, which have various sizes of physical asset collections, such as works of art, clothing, or artifacts, and need a system to manage them. Because museums often lend or borrow items and collections, they also need to capture a variety of information around the physical asset, including the name of the artist or discoverer, the history of the asset, the relationship to other assets or geographic locations or to a specific collection of items, and the loan history. Sometimes this is done separately in a collection management system (the museum world's CMS), but increasingly, DAM systems are used to store this data. A museum archive requires more involved metadata modeling, detailing relationships among assets, metadata, and possibly folders, as well as multivalued relationships (one to many, many to one, and many to many). If collections data is kept separately in the aforementioned CMS, DAM use cases at museums almost always involve interfacing to that sophisticated (and dedicated) collection management software.

This same use case can describe a seemingly simple photo "management" scenario, yet this use case can develop into a highly profitable business model. The ability to preset images for sale or licensing (and many e-commerce systems today can manage the fulfillment aspects) can grow from a simple, photo-management style DAM to a profitable business. See Table 10.1 for further examples.

Scenario 2: Brand-Centric Asset Management

Every company has a brand or product to manage. Corporate communications and marketing departments use the brand library to store and find common brand elements, logos, style guides, documentation, and finished pieces. You may share those assets with both internal teams and external agencies and partners. In some instances, you may focus on a single asset type, such as cataloging all logos or online banner ads.

TABLE 10.1   DAM LIBRARY OR PHOTO ARCHIVE

Information Model	Basic metadata for simple cataloging, search, and retrieval; for museums, more advanced metadata modeling including relationships among assets, metadata and groups of assets, multivalued relationships and metadata fields, and potentially inherited metadata (from a group of assets representing a collection).
Workflows	• Simple cataloging and ingestion workflows to facilitate easier end-user search • Ability to revise and add information over time and track revisions • High-volume photo archives that may require streamlining for ingestion • Basic to advanced content tagging • Sharing via lightboxes and showcases
Functional Emphasis	• Metadata extraction, bulk ingestion • Metadata modeling and information capture • Simple metadata search • Descriptive metadata with an understanding of end-user access patterns • Ability to group and relate assets • Basic security • SaaS or installed
Typical Adopters	• Media companies • Stock photo and image agencies • Ad agencies • Small company marketing groups • Manufacturers with useful image and/or design archives • Colleges or universities • Museums
System Modifications	Minimal to none—configuration by novice marketing person, novice IT staffer, or outside consultant; museums may require advanced modification for the metadata model and integration into an existing collection management system; minimal potential integration with an e-commerce system.

Simple brand management requires basic metadata support, basic packaged transformations to provide approved renditions for various media, security to control asset access and visibility, and a simple folder structure to facilitate navigation and search across brands. You also need basic website integration—perhaps via asset URL reference—that supports presenting specific images or brochures in pages on a corporate website or extranet. The system should also support "Google-like" search, as well as search over a limited set of metadata fields. Over time or in larger organizations, the system may evolve into midrange channel or distribution management as it incorporates external users. In those scenarios, you will need deeper support for the security model, search, metadata, and geographic distribution, so the DAM system must be scalable and provide that extra support without additional software licensing costs. See Table 10.2 for further examples.

Scenario 3: Multilingual Brand Management

Multilingual brand management is like simple brand management, except that it adds on the need to support simultaneous access to the same assets in multiple languages. As such, every piece of metadata for every asset must exist in all the languages required by the installation. The DAM system not only must support a multilingual metadata model at the asset level but also has to support workflows for creating and maintaining that metadata in all the necessary languages.

As discussed earlier, DAM system support for multilingual metadata goes far beyond internationalization. Internationalization means that the DAM system can support the user experience in another language. Typically, the screens, label names, error messages, and input fields support the language of choice. It doesn't necessarily mean that the DAM system can support a metadata model in which every metadata field can have N different values of both the field name and field value, where N is the number of simultaneous languages used to access the DAM system. To support a multilingual metadata model, the DAM system needs to provide every experience in the language of choice. Further, it must support a metadata model that allows for a metadata field that can exist in multiple languages simultaneously.

For instance, if the "Name" metadata field for a photo asset in English is "A black cat," in Spanish the same field is "Nombre," and the value is "Un gato negro." It would be the same for French, German, and every other supported language. Further, the DAM system can support searches only in the chosen language. A search for "gato negro" would

TABLE 10.2 BRAND-CENTRIC ASSET MANAGEMENT

Information Model	Basic descriptive metadata for simple cataloging, search and retrieval, and document text used for full-text search.
	"Where used" relationship—Determine what compound documents use which assets (with special consideration in the case of branding and logos).
Workflows	• Simple cataloging to facilitate easier end-user search • Metadata revision and versioning of assets • Significant revision control—Add information over time, version assets, version compound assets, coordinate related assets • Flexible security—Light for internal use, stronger for intercompany/agency use • Tracking and reporting on downloads and asset usage
Functional Emphasis	• Descriptive metadata, with an understanding of end-user access patterns • Parametric metadata search across individual fields • Consistent and well-tested navigational folder structure • Compound asset support—Adobe Illustrator, Adobe InDesign, Web to Print (W2P) • Brand guidelines tool to maintain brand consistency • Basic security • Asset download and access tracking and reporting • Web access and browser based • SaaS or installed
Typical Adopters	• Manufacturing companies • Retail, hospitality, and consumer product companies • Companies with national or global brands, including media companies (such as studios and publishers) • Corporate and traditional marketing departments • Individual brands within large multibrand company • Large multibrand companies that need multiple brand portals • Ad agencies • Nonprofits and academic institutions with logos and related assets
System Modifications	Minimal—Mostly the metadata model, taxonomy, navigational structures, or folders and security model, which is the standard setup for any DAM use case.
	The more workflow and "brand guidelines" needed means that the system requires greater modification than simpler branding scenarios require. A novice user with some vendor assistance or training should be able to perform these functions. Some assistance might be needed for integration to an external workflow system.

yield those assets that matched the criteria, while someone else search-ing for "black cat" would get the same results. As you walk through this example, you get a feel for the potential workflow challenge of entering and maintaining the same metadata in multiple languages. Any change in any language may require a change in all languages. As a result, multilingual brand management becomes significantly more challenging, both for the multilingual metadata requirements and the potential corresponding localization workflows.

Companies in regulated industries (beyond labeling) have more pronounced requirements. These include companies such as pharma-ceutical and medical device makers, others where "indelible" audit trails are critical (such as avionics parts manufacturing and repair where versioning by part and revision level is required by law), and industries where poor translation can lead to embarrassing situa-tions (in movie subtitles, for example). These all require an elaborate approval queue and audit trail common to multilingual brand management scenarios.

All the other characteristics of the simple brand management sce-nario also apply (see Table 10.3).

Scenario 4: Advertising and Marketing Asset Management

Many enterprises use DAM as the authoritative source for market-ing and brand content. It becomes the single source of this material for direct distribution to internal and external stakeholders, either directly as DAM system users, or indirectly through a portal, web-site, or other distribution application.

Marketing groups commonly create and assemble marketing col-lateral in conjunction with internal or external design or creative groups. Ad agencies and design groups often create print advertising as part of a marketing campaign. The core of this effort is the creative workflow, which includes creating or accessing assets to incorporate into a new design or layout document and iteratively reviewing the process with the client.

This workflow may require multiple variations of the ad, each repre-senting a different idea, or presenting the same idea with a different theme. It may require access to stock photos, stock video, and specific images, as well as to textual copy, brand imagery, and logos. You must manage all of these assets and versions of the ad.

TABLE 10.3 MULTILINGUAL BRAND MANAGEMENT

Information Model	Basic descriptive metadata for simple cataloging, search and retrieval, and document text used for full-text search, but with multiple languages supported simultaneously for both metadata and full-text search.
Workflows	• Multilingual metadata input, review, approval, and modification • Fundamentally simple cataloging, except that now it has to be done in multiple languages • Metadata revision and versioning of assets—now with support for multiple languages as well • Tracking and reporting on downloads and asset usage
Functional Emphasis	• Multilingual metadata support • Multilingual search and presentation • Multilingual workflows • Descriptive metadata with understanding of end-user access patterns • Parametric metadata search across individual fields • Consistent and well-tested navigational folder structure (also in multiple languages) • Basic security • Asset download and access tracking and reporting • Web access and browser based • SaaS or installed
Typical Adopters	• Manufacturing companies • Retail, hospitality, and consumer product companies • Companies with national or global brands • Corporate and traditional marketing departments • Individual brands within a large multibrand company • Ad agencies • Certain governmental agencies (such as the UN and EU oversight bodies)
System Modifications	Modification is minimal if the system supports multilingual metadata. The challenge is in maintaining the multilingual metadata model, taxonomy, navigational structures, or folders—and whether the system facilitates that out of the box. If so, it becomes a workflow issue and not a technical issue.

This effort may require creating multiple pieces of marketing collateral simultaneously or in parallel, and there may be significant shared copy and assets between the pieces. You need to track the status and maintain the relationships between related assets, as well as gain access to stock photos and specific images.

This process requires significant project management, coordination, scheduling, and asset sharing. Workflow is typically external to most DAM systems. If there is no internal workflow in the DAM system, you will need to integrate it with an external workflow engine or tool.

The ability to set up groups/folders/collections of assets and selectively share access, perhaps at different times with different people, will facilitate the production process. You may also want scheduling, completion notification, and review/approval process management. Therefore, a workflow engine becomes highly desirable. Depending on the size of the company and number of products to launch, tracking the process can entail significant effort.

The DAM system needs a light security model that allows internal and external asset sharing while maintaining proper isolation of projects, workflows, and access to assets. Some of the collateral pieces will be expressed as a compound asset, so the system must support and integrate with Illustrator, InDesign, Photoshop, and possibly Final Cut Pro. Version control helps manage both in-process revisions and released versions of finished goods. Other useful functions include the ability to track the "where used" relationship; to manage rights on stock photos/video; and to handle finished assets that span a range from Word and PDF files to PowerPoint presentations, advertisements, and videos.

Creatives like to stay inside their tools. They want minimal interruption or hindrances to their creative process and efforts. Using a DAM system is generally foreign to them. They don't want to be bothered with adding metadata to the asset or leaving their tools or environment to upload, package, store, or find assets. Therefore, they require deep integration between the DAM system and the creative tools and environments, such as Mac Finder or Windows Explorer.

Print ads and video ads (more on these later) are compound documents or compound assets. Creatives must be able to work with a compound asset, upload it, and download it—without the need to "Package for Output" from the creative tool and manually store it in the DAM system. They need to version the asset, version assets within it, and manage a configuration of a compound asset and its content over time. The system must support Adobe Creative Suite (that is, InDesign, Illustrator, and Photoshop), for storage and integration with the tool or environment to facilitate access to the DAM system.

Distribution takes on various flavors. The DAM system, through a web interface, becomes a sales and marketing distribution portal providing common and consistent access to approved materials, logos, photographs, and artwork to approved external users. Following are some examples:

- Media companies use a DAM system for electronic press kits (EPKs) to distribute photographs, posters, video clips, or promotional materials of upcoming shows to media outlets, ad agencies, and Web properties.

- A manufacturer distributes product information to its WCM-based sites, portals, or partner websites and distributes it securely and directly to distributed sales and marketing teams around the globe for use in their regional catalogs. The manufacturer embargoes assets until the launch date, at which point they become available to specific populations.

- A consumer brand provides specific assets to its distributors or retailers for their brochures, circulars, or video advertising. Assets expire within the system when they are no longer usable.

- A drug manufacturer establishes an internal portal for each drug brand. Each portal provides that brand's distributed global sales and marketing teams with common access to the approved marketing materials. Assets can be both embargoed and expired as necessary.

- An ad agency helps its field marketing representatives create localized advertisements for its clients using approved brand content.

In all of these instances, the DAM system acts as the single source of approved brand and marketing materials, and distributes them only to approved parties. It is not for commerce or sale. Content is organized into consistent folder structures that facilitate ease of adoption, quick learning, and consistent navigation. The system has basic, consistent metadata and Google-like quick search across both metadata and the text of documents. It includes role-based security, support of users and groups, and the ability to apply security to specific assets.

Additional requirements include the ability to email links to assets; to select, zip, and download assets; to transform assets; and to transform assets automatically prior to distribution or delivery.

Some fulfillment may occur by invoking other output formats, such as large-scale printing for banners or DVD pressing due to large file sizes or remote locations without a broadband infrastructure.

The system should provide notification of new or updated assets or subscription to assets. It should support embargo and expiration workflows, either making the asset available to a defined set of users based on specific criteria, such as the date, or removing or restricting access to a defined set of users based on specific criteria. Metadata fields contain basic usage rights, which these workflows use to determine the expiration or embargo criteria. These workflows can be both manual and automated. Automated workflows tend to be more powerful and useful. Being able to manage the usage rights attached to assets gives marketing and brand managers greater control over asset distribution to appropriate users.

We distinguish usage rights into two general categories:

- **Channel management:** Internal distribution, such as an ad agency to its field reps, a company to its regional marketing and internal sales teams, or globally for internal product launches. Another variation is managing the content that is distributed to different media channels, including Web, print, mobile, and cable.

- **Distribution management:** Externally focused distribution to partners, distributors, and suppliers, perhaps on a global basis. Security needs expand because now you have outside-of-company users. Distribution management can include pushing assets or pushing on-the-fly transformed assets to partner sites. It also includes syndication of branded material to partner sites, Web properties, and content distribution networks (CDNs) such as Akamai and Brightcove. For this latter case, the DAM system needs to be able to integrate with or push content to the CDN. If this type of external collaboration is in your workflow stack, we strongly encourage you to try to model it in your own scenarios so the prospective vendors can gain insight into these operations.

Campaigns involving video assets introduce another level of complexity to the workflows, particularly if collaborative editing and annotation are involved. The more important that tracking campaign efficacy is (or smaller unit of granularity it has), the more essential it is that assets are tagged or carry a digital identifier to achieve the desired levels of analytics. Although digital rights assignment software that's outside the DAM can imprint or "stamp" assets, if this is important to you, it should be required as part of a vendor's abilities.

We also want to comment briefly on packaging development and the sometimes-specialized software that supports these workflows. Requirements vary from fairly simple and straightforward concepts, to approval (for example, game packaging, where the parental guidance "rating" may be the most stringent requirement and it's mostly just creative), or heavily regulated drug and food packaging. The advent of QR codes, Internet of Things, and embedded object-based augmented reality may reinforce the importance of such requirements.

Some packaging software includes lightweight DAM functionality. For a more sophisticated and efficient approach, some DAM vendors have prebuilt integrations with these tools. If your company already uses these or other prepress utilities, be certain that your assessments include scenarios derived from them, so the DAM can become the central content management tool (see Table 10.4).

TABLE 10.4 ADVERTISING AND MARKETING ASSET MANAGEMENT

Information Model	• Basic descriptive metadata for simple cataloging, search, and retrieval; well-structured folder hierarchy for consistent navigational access
	• Simple descriptive metadata will suffice for most assets; however, information from PIM or integrated marketing platforms may be used to supplement
	• "Where used" relationship—to determine which compound documents use which assets
Workflows	• Many overlapping and parallel create-review-edit-review-approve creative workflows
	• Simple cataloging to facilitate easier creative search and transparent access to DAM from creative tools
	• Automated text indexing
	• Asset selection, grouping assets into projects, project tracking
	• Significant revision control—add information over time, version assets, version compound assets, coordinate related assets
	• Basic content tagging
	• Adequate notification utility
	• Optional embargo and expiration workflows
	• Distribution workflows—assigning assets for access by groups of users
	• Potential synchronization workflows to sync changes made to the same content in different channel workflows
	• Optional transformation workflows prior to distribution

continues on next page

TABLE 10.4 ADVERTISING AND MARKETING ASSET MANAGEMENT (*continued*)

Functional Emphasis	• Simple descriptive metadata and easy-to-use search • Google-like search for both metadata and full text • Deeper integration with creative tools—invisible/transparent access to DAM • Compound asset support—Adobe InDesign, Illustrator • Potential for integration to external workflow systems and to CDNs • Basic security and access control to support, review, and approval workflows • Asset transformation • Features supporting expiration and embargo workflows • Robust workflow, project management, scheduling support • Multiparty review and approval • Deeper integration with creative tools—invisible/transparent access to DAM • Compound asset support—Adobe Illustrator, Adobe InDesign • Basic versioning with compound asset versioning • Access to asset versions from within creative tools • Group and relate assets and projects • Methods by which marketing campaigns can be set up and presented with showcasing tools • Flexible security—light for internal use, stronger for intercompany/agency use • Web access and browser based • SaaS or installed
Typical Adopters	• Corporate communications • Brand managers • Marketing organizations • Internal services groups • Ad agencies • Corporate marketing • Marketing departments • Individual brands within large multibrand company
System Modifications	Light to heavy—Primarily for workflow and, if needed, workflow engine integration and workflow process definition. Setup of the metadata/information model, users/roles/groups, appropriate security configuration, and basic workflows to support the basic review/approval workflow. A novice user with some vendor assistance or training should be able to perform these functions. Some assistance might be needed if the system is integrated to an external workflow system. Integrations with marketing platforms and PIM might be necessary depending on the use case.

Publishing

A team of people creates a new asset, such as a brochure or a 30-second spot, and needs to store this work in progress (WIP) in an interim place to provide common access and potentially to sequence the work. This is the generic idea. There can be very specialized WIP scenarios, with particular workflows and interactions between users, tools, and the DAM system, and integration with additional tools or systems.

Scenario 5: Periodical and Catalog Production and Management

While periodical production has many common processes and assets, each publication has its own distinct style and layout and its own creative, editorial, and production workflows.

Magazine production requires orchestrating multiple authors, editors, photographers, advertising reps, and others on a firm deadline. Magazines place a heavy emphasis on workflow, scheduling, coordination, and tracking. Typically, publishers manage this process in a publishing, editorial, or workflow system, such as SoftCare GmbH's K4, WoodWing, or (more rarely) Quark Publishing System, that is external to the DAM system. To date, we haven't seen deep integrations between these systems and the DAM systems, despite the obvious need. Neither have we seen integration between these two systems and the creative tools, although some kind of integration is necessary. The DAM system might also integrate with an ad layout system (ALS), ad booking system, or billing system.

In some cases, the DAM system is an afterthought, where the magazine archives and indexes the final version. In an increasing number of cases, however, the DAM system plays an integral role in the workflow for storing the magazine and its in-process versions, and all the individual assets—photos, copy, advertising, layout documents, Word documents, and templates.

We've seen a recent interest to produce for the Web, for mobile, and for print using common assets expressed differently to the different media. The system should be able to transform photos from Web to print formats or vice versa, and now increasingly to mobile, tablets, and the like. Essential functions include supporting multipage compound assets, tracking where an asset is used within a compound asset, and managing versions of compound assets and assets.

Additionally, the system should have a basic security model, full-text and metadata field search, and representational support in the metadata model for PRISM data.

Within magazine publishing, a number of specific scenarios involve either managing specific types of content, with related yet refined workflows, or creating special, annual, topical, or customized editions. A DAM system performs well in all of these scenarios.

The production of annual or customized publications has some unique needs. In this scenario, the publisher uses existing assets in the development and publication of more narrowly focused books or magazines. For example, *Reptiles of the World* might be an initial publication, whereas *Reptiles of North America* or *Snakes of the United States* would be narrower publications with much of the same content, copy, images, and assets. Similar scenarios include textbooks that include or exclude content depending on the region; focused magazines targeting a specific demographic or single topic, in which some or all of the content has been drawn from earlier published editions; and regional magazines, which have a similar layout but are content-specific to a region, country, or section of a country.

In all of these examples, you need to be able to search and copy assets, based on both metadata and full-text search. Knowing what content was used where is also important. You may also need copyright and usage information. This scenario places less emphasis on the security model and version control. While there is some editorial workflow, it is predominantly review and approval, with the copy editor accessing DAM system content from within the creative tools, which facilitates the creative's job in laying out the magazine or book.

Producing weekly features or elements, such as the Sunday comic section, is another highly specialized form of production. You need to work with a significant amount of time-sensitive editorial workflow, from receiving the original comic strip artwork to editing to final approval, At that point, the system must prepare the element for syndication, distribute it to media outlets, and ultimately archive it. You need many of the functions we've highlighted previously: project management, workflow management, review and approval, versioning, proper access to content, and seamless integration with creative tools as well as with Microsoft Word. Over the long term, this scenario focuses on archiving, so the additional archival scenario requirements also apply.

The further the reach of the DAM system to these editorial and production workflows, the more important the conversation with the vendor is about its ability to integrate with contemporary subscription and point-of-purchase tools, such as SAP's Consume to Cash. Content products may be measured and monetized at the article, author, topic, issue, or device level, and the ability of the DAM system to support this is increasingly important. The interface to royalty streams will also emerge in importance.

Similarly, producing and publishing an online or print catalog can be a complex DAM application because it typically draws only some of its information from a DAM system, such as the product images and photographs. The remainder of the product data may come from a product data management (PDM) system, a database, or multiple systems.

While enterprises historically produced only a print catalog, now almost all of them develop identical print and online versions of the catalog (or store circular). In many cases, the print catalog converts into a PDF document and can be posted as an online catalog using third-party software. PDF documents can be stored in the DAM system, but the system needs to be able to support the storage of the original multipage compound documents. This implementation is complex because the system must both support the multipage compound documents and integrate into external database and product data management systems.

To support multipage documents, the DAM system may need to integrate with publishing or workflow engines, such as SoftCare's K4 or WoodWing. Additionally, it may need to coordinate the workflows, especially if multiple authors require multiple reviews and approvals. It should also integrate with a layout tool, typically Adobe InDesign.

Newer, dynamic publishing catalog systems can integrate with DAM and PDM systems, as well as databases to provide a comprehensive off-the-shelf catalog development system. You may need multiple renditions of images for print or online catalogs, or dynamic image cropping, rotating, resizing, or image composing (such as "50% Off" in a starburst graphic overlaid on the image). See Table 10.5 for further details.

TABLE 10.5 PERIODICAL AND CATALOG PRODUCTION AND
MANAGEMENT

Information Model	• Basic descriptive metadata for simple cataloging and image search and retrieval, text copy accessed via full-text search
	• "Where used" relationship—determines which compound documents use which assets
	• For catalogs, simple or advanced metadata may include product and SKU data or may have multiple images per SKU or multiple related SKUs and images. They may also have a navigational structure organizing product lines
Workflows	• Many parallel selection and review-edit-review-approve creative workflows
	• Content tagging for later access and search DAM from within creative tools
	• Basic to advanced content tagging for product images
	• Automated text indexing
	• Asset selection and grouping into projects
	• Significant revision control—add information over time, version assets, version compound assets, coordinate related assets
	• Coordination via external editorial or workflow systems
	• Multiple review and approval workflow for approving product data, images, pages, and so on, possibly coordinated by the external workflow or publishing system
	• Optional transformation workflows prior to layout
	• Integration with and access from common layout and design tools
	• Cleaning or scrubbing product definition data in the PDM to the images or assets is part of the problem but not part of the DAM system workflow

TABLE 10.5 PERIODICAL AND CATALOG PRODUCTION AND MANAGEMENT (*continued*)

Functional Emphasis	• Integration to external workflow and editorial systems, possibly to ad booking, ALS, and billing systems
	• Security and access control supporting parallel review approval workflows
	• Basic versioning with compound asset versioning
	• Simple descriptive metadata, easy-to-use search, full-text search
	• Web access and browser based
	• Deep compound asset support—multipage document storage, retrieval, and versioning requirements
	• Deeper integration with desktop creative tools—invisible/transparent access to DAM from layout tools
	• Security and access control supporting parallel review approval workflows
	• Ability to group and relate assets and product definition data
	• Possible product family-centric folder structures
	• "Where used" relationship—ability to determine which compound documents use which assets
	• Search for both metadata and full text
	• Asset transformation
	• SaaS or installed
	• Manufacturing companies
	• Content or product aggregators
	• Traditional print catalog companies
Typical Adopters	• Publishers
	• Corporate communications
	• Internal corporate publication groups
	• Retailers
System Modifications	Medium to heavy—primarily for editorial and workflow system integration. More advanced for catalogs—setup of the metadata/information model to be coordinated with and integrated to external PDM, database, and other systems containing product data; additional integration with an external workflow or publishing system, as well as design tools—lead to complex workflows.

Scenario 6: Multichannel Publishing

Multichannel publishing implies that you're publishing similar or the same content across multiple channels or media simultaneously with different workflows, lead times, formatting, and requirements. For instance, simultaneously publishing the same content to print, Web, and mobile (including tablets) can be a tremendously complex process. You must coordinate the different workflows, tools, and teams of people. You need to track and coordinate assets and content across multiple different workflows and output formats. Moreover, you must integrate multiple systems.

Multichannel publishing assumes a single source for all the content, so a DAM system is an appropriate solution. It also requires that the content and text be single sourced. Depending on the business requirements, an XML database may be a better fit than a DAM system for heavy-duty single source content management. Additional challenges include global asset identification across systems and integration with other systems, such as product data management Systems and websites. Further, the system must coordinate changes to assets and relationships between assets and compound assets across the different workflows.

Publishers such as Hearst and Time, Inc., broadcasters such as WWE and HBO, and retailers such as JCPenney, Lands' End, and Skechers are great examples of multichannel publishers. JCPenney has a multichannel publishing strategy—on mobile, website, in circulars, and in stores—and it all must be the same. The emerging content environment for the mobile user—screen savers, ring tones, games, full websites, and mobile applications—adds to the complexity. You face management on a massive scale of lots of little chunks of content, from many providers, each with different rights bundles, and offered to millions of users.

These highly specialized systems must manage both the volume of content from a variety of suppliers and a variety of complex relationships among assets, devices, providers, consumers, and rights definitions at multiple levels. From a workflow perspective, the application must feature multistep content aggregation, metadata entry, and validation processes, including content format validation and content testing.

Almost any company that publishes any type of instruction manual or "do-it-yourself" guide has become a multichannel publisher, even if it sells cars or decking materials as a primary source of revenue.

As you select from these scenarios and develop your own, remember that you will need to address many organizational changes in tandem with the increased resources that are required to become a multichannel publisher.

Adding to the complexity and demands on the system is the need to support infrastructure for mobile content transformation—every device has different requirements—and content billing and distribution through the carrier's website and distribution infrastructure. The system must be able to interoperate with many third-party systems. In addition to tracking the rights and relationships of content bundles, the system must be able to transform content into a wide variety of device-specific formats and to adapt to new devices as they enter the market. While an indirect concern of DAM, companies realizing revenue through numerous digital outlets will require audit and revenue assurance interventions as governance committees begin to request this information. Table 10.6 provides further details.

TABLE 10.6 MULTICHANNEL PUBLISHING

Information Model	Typically simple descriptive metadata for most assets; however, the management of text may require an additional external data management system (for example, an XML database) to support single sourcing, plus an additional metadata model for rights management information.
	A focus on delivering information in nonpublished formats, with more of a focus on integrating with e-commerce and ordering platforms as well as taking into account the importance of video content.
Workflows	• Complex, multiple separate workflows and teams for content acquisition, normalization, tagging, transcoding, transformation, reporting, accounting, distribution, validation, and testing
	• Multiple review and approval workflows for approving content for each channel, and accuracy or consistency across channels possibly coordinated by external workflow or publishing system
	• Basic to advanced content tagging
	• Optional transformation workflows prior to layout
	• Integration with and access from common layout and design tools
	• Potential synchronization workflows to sync changes made to the same content in different channel workflows

continues on next page

TABLE 10.6 MULTICHANNEL PUBLISHING (*continued*)

Workflows (*continued*)	• Workflows for content providers, maintainers, and tracking • Detailed embargo and expiration workflows with control over both process and execution • Workflows extend further than those that are focused on asset creation and delivery, extending into real-world situations where assets represent a physical entity that is to be delivered or sold
Functional Emphasis	• Compound asset support—multipage document storage, retrieval, and versioning requirements • Relationships among assets, including "where used" to determine assets used in which compound assets • Deeper integration with desktop creative tools—invisible/transparent access to DAM from Adobe InDesign, Illustrator, and Apple Final Cut Pro • Potential integration to external workflow, publishing, and WCM systems • Potential integration to XML databases and authoring tools • Security and access control supporting parallel review approval workflows • Basic versioning but support for compound-asset versioning, also with access to asset versions from within creative tools • Ability to group and relate assets • Basic to advanced metadata • Web access and browser based • Asset transformation • SaaS or installed • Advanced rights management metadata model • Google-like search for both metadata and full text • Ability to manipulate rights and content bundle definitions and relationships • Integration to external workflow systems, CDNs, back-office systems, e-commerce systems, and end-user portals • Advanced security and access control to support embargo, expiration, review, and approval workflows, with access by multiple groups of external users (content providers, consumers) • Digital rights management (DRM) support—integration with DRM systems • Flexible, broad asset transformation • Deep reporting support for content providers and suppliers • Integration to e-commerce/ordering systems

TABLE 10.6   MULTICHANNEL PUBLISHING (*continued*)

Typical Adopters	• Publishing companies
	• Advertisers
	• Retailers
	• Manufacturing companies
	• Marketing departments
	• Pharmaceutical companies
	• Media companies
	• Content aggregators
	• E-commerce
System Modifications	Advanced—integration and coordination with external systems (XML databases, workflow or publishing systems, WCM, and so on) as well as design tools—lead to complex workflows that also require coordination and may require content synchronization for accuracy and brand consistency. Monitoring workflow across different channels is a challenge.
	Integration and coordination with external systems (e-commerce, PIM).

Corporate Time-Based Media Management

For an enterprise, one of the most common starting points and basic uses of a DAM system is as a media asset library. In this scenario, your DAM system functions as a common, centralized place to catalog and store all video and assorted assets.

Some companies start with an inexpensive, hosted consumer service like YouTube or Vimeo to get a centralized corporate video library up and running. However, don't expect customer service to have much flexibility integrating with your internal video-editing suites, facilitating highly granular role and group permissions management, or distributing high-resolution broadcast-quality assets. Web-based, consumer-oriented tools are just that—made for consumers and the Web.

This technology primarily is adopted by advertising agencies, corporate marketing groups, and other organizations creating exclusively "born digital" media. Part of this scenario is "point of presence" video creation and management, such as digital billboards and informational videos playing in stores, building lobbies, kiosks, or security checkpoints.

Scenario 7: Audio and Video Library Review and Approval

Audio and video library review and approval is the first—and simplest—of the time-based media scenarios. Your marketing or audio/video production team works collaboratively with an ad agency or production studio to produce audio or video for corporate, marketing, or promotional use. This scenario occurs regularly in the marketing departments of many enterprises, including traditional entertainment and media companies. Colleges and universities use it to provide rich media materials for prospective students or as an e-learning module.

These materials are not created in the DAM system but are often put into it so that they can be reviewed and approved by clients or third parties. As such, this scenario doesn't involve the higher-end audio- and video-editing functionality that's required in other scenarios. Essentially, the DAM system becomes a repository for audio and video files and helps manage the workflow among the various team members. The system can store a combination of raw footage and video clips.

Rather than passing video clips around via email, or having to log in to an FTP site to retrieve and view a clip, you use the DAM system to share these video files. You use the system to move, upload, store, review, annotate, and transfer clips and video works. In this case, you're using the DAM system only to facilitate the review process; you're not using it to select material and fashion it into clips.

In this workflow, the DAM system only has to support basic video capabilities:

- Upload video and audio files

- Enter basic metadata about the files

- Allow for versions of the files

- Make the files available to specific people on your team, using either the security model or the security model combined with shared folders

- Allow users to download and view the files

- Allow users to make annotations to metadata or directly on the video itself for later review

- Capture whether a video has been approved, which can be captured in metadata

While a workflow engine can facilitate and speed the process, it's not an absolute requirement for the DAM system to support this scenario. You will need the ability to play the video or audio—most players support the ability to start it at any point—and capture your comments on it. Allowing for purely browser-based playback (rather than download and playback) is a nice feature but not necessarily a requirement. Note that this playback feature can add complexity to the back end because you would need a streaming server and additional storage for streamed files. The ability to email links to assets from the DAM system greatly facilitates this scenario.

For the simplest form of this scenario, you don't need advanced features like scene detection, time code extraction, speech-to-text, the ability to play from a specific time code or frame in a video, or clip creation features. These features add more editing capabilities, moving away from simple review and approval to a more powerful and complex audio/video production and editing scenario.

The digital daily scenario is almost identical to the video review and approval scenario, except that it applies specifically to media and entertainment companies. A "digital daily" represents a snapshot of an in-process movie or video production work that's shared among the production team and corporate executives.

In this scenario, the DAM system becomes a repository for audio and video and helps manage the review among production and executive reviewers. The system can store a combination of raw footage, clips, and the digital daily in various stages and digital forms. Rather than passing around videotapes, sending the digital daily by email, or logging in to an FTP site, the production team uses the DAM system as the vehicle for sharing and communicating digital dailies. The system can move, upload, store, review, annotate, and transfer digital dailies. It provides a secure, controlled, and integrated environment for reviewing the digital daily. This can be one of several applications using the DAM system as part of your enterprise's overall digital asset infrastructure. It is a short step from here to using the DAM for the workflows around trailers and publicity materials.

Many workflows now require that video can be viewed on tablets and approved, even in this simple scenario. An ad sales rep may show a car dealer a "spot" for TV or the Web; a producer may approve a rough cut. Whatever the case, your system should be able to incorporate mobile tablet action steps.

In this workflow, the DAM system only has to support basic video capabilities:

- Upload video files

- Enter basic metadata about the files

- Allow for versions of the files

- Make the files available to specific people on your team, using the security model or the security model combined with shared folders

- Allow users to download and view the files

- Allow users to make annotations to metadata or directly on the video itself for later review

- Capture whether or not a video has been approved, which can be captured in metadata

Lastly, you easily can implement this scenario in a SaaS model, where the system is hosted by the vendor or by a vendor's cloud partner. This can lower your overall expense, and it fits well into traditional marketing budgets as a monthly operational expense. The system can be an installed, in-house solution. The on-site DAM system could have many functions in your organization, especially if you have made a strategic commitment to a digital infrastructure for the production, sharing, and distribution of digital assets. See Table 10.7 for further details.

Scenario 8: Audio and Video Production and Reuse

Scenario 8, Audio and Video Production and Reuse, focuses on the creation or production of audio or video in the corporate or ad agency environment. It usually refers to commercials, advertisements, radio broadcasts, or promotional video ranging from 15 seconds to a few minutes long. This type of audio and video has become common in organizations that use these media for corporate, marketing, or product communication. This scenario moves beyond simple review and approval to bring the DAM system into the middle of A/V production and editing workflows.

As in the prior scenario, the DAM system serves as a repository for audio and video and helps manage the review between production and reviewers. Again, the DAM system can store a combination

TABLE 10.7 AUDIO AND VIDEO LIBRARY REVIEW AND APPROVAL

Information Model	Basic descriptive metadata for simple cataloging, search and retrieval, and metadata search to find specific audio or video files.
Workflows	• Basic review-approve workflows • Basic file metadata workflows—extraction and later modification and annotation • Asset selection and grouping assets into projects • Controlled workflows with check-in/check-out and revision control—add information over time, version video assets • Potential coordination with external workflow systems • Potential migration to video-editing and review workflows and integration with video-editing tools • Streamlining will most likely be required for large-media file ingestion • Basic to advanced content tagging
Functional Emphasis	• Basic audio and video support with a focus on video review and approval • Security and access control supporting parallel review approval workflows • Basic versioning • Ability to group and relate assets and projects • Ability to email links to assets • Simple descriptive metadata, with easy-to-use search • Web access, browser, and possibly app based • SaaS or installed on-site • Descriptive metadata with an understanding of end-user access patterns • A/V search and preview and support for storyboards
Typical Adopters	• Corporate communications • Corporate marketing • Ad agencies • Radio stations • Media and entertainment companies • Media, marketing, and entertainment companies
System Modifications	Minimal—A novice user with some vendor assistance or training should be able to set up the metadata/information model, users/roles/groups, appropriate security configuration, and basic workflows to support the basic review and approval workflow. A streaming engine may be required, depending on the quality of previews required of A/V on the system.

of raw footage, clips, and works in progress at various stages and digital forms. Rather than passing around videotapes, sending clips by email, or logging in to an FTP site to retrieve and view the video, you use the DAM system as the vehicle for sharing and communicating. You use it to move, upload, store, review, annotate, and transfer audio and video clips and works in progress. It provides a secure, controlled, and integrated environment to review the audio or video. This can be one of several applications using the DAM system as part of your enterprise's overall digital asset infrastructure.

Unlike the prior scenario, however, the DAM system in this workflow is more capable and provides significantly deeper support for finding, selecting, editing, reviewing, preparing, and distributing A/V content. The system ingests audio and video more deeply and extracts more information from it than simply the metadata about the video file.

Deeper audio and video support for this scenario includes the following:

- Extracting key frames and time codes from A/V files for quick visual identification, particularly of video content.

- Presenting key frames in the user interface for video in a "storyboard"—a linear sequence that roughly shows the video content flow.

- Visually displaying the first few words of an audio clip.

- Extracting existing audio as text, or transcribing closed-caption text—if it occurs—with time codes and indexes of that text to the time code or frame in the audio or video file, mapping where the spoken words occur.

- Playing a file from any point or frame in the file that you select, implying support for an A/V streaming server as part of the core configuration. This also implies that it can be done entirely within a browser.

- Converting speech into text, specifically into a text transcript with the text indexed to the particular frame in which the spoken words occur, thus allowing searching for video frames or audio clips by full-text search.

- Defining video and audio "clips," which are segments of video or audio defined by a start frame and end frame. They also can be defined by start and end time, in which case they are called "in and out points."

- Naming of clips for easy retrieval.

- Saving the clips as new assets, which may imply that the system copies the new clip out of the file and makes it into a new asset with a new asset ID.

- Creating a clip list, or edit decision list (EDL), from multiple clips from the same source file, thereby providing a "rough cut" or "rough edit" of an A/V sequence.

- "Conforming" a clip list or EDL into a new asset, which entails taking a clip list and forming a new asset composed of the clips in the sequence as they exist in the clip list.

- Annotating the A/V file by adding textual or graphical notations and associating them to video frames or A/V time codes.

- Integrating with A/V editing environments including Avid, Audacity, and Final Cut Pro, so that access to the DAM system and the ability to search for audio or video are available from these environments, or the DAM system can format and deliver video for editing in an automated fashion. These environments can also easily submit and upload edited video back to the DAM system for review, approval, distribution, and other workflows.

If the DAM system can facilitate working with clips, it makes the process easier for both novice and experienced A/V editors because it allows unsophisticated users to use the DAM system to search for, select, and assemble rough selections of A/V clips that can be refined and finished by an experienced editor. This scenario distributes the A/V workload and empowers traditional marketers to become more active in the selection, editing, and review processes in a nontechnical manner.

The DAM system has to support these basic A/V capabilities:

- Upload A/V files

- Enter basic metadata about the files

- Allow for versions of the files

- Make the files available to specific people on your team, using the security model or the security model combined with shared folders

- Allow users to download and view the files

- Allow users to make annotations to metadata or directly on video itself for later review

- Capture whether or not an A/V file has been approved, which can be captured in metadata

As before, while a workflow engine would certainly facilitate the broader selection, production, review, and distribution processes, it's not an absolute requirement for the DAM system to support this scenario. You will need the ability to play the audio and video—and most players support the ability to start at any point in the file—and capture your comments on it. The DAM system's ability to email links to assets can greatly facilitate this scenario.

As discussed much earlier, however, you may have capacity concerns for ingesting and transcoding data, depending on the scale of this scenario in your organization. If you have many small A/V files arriving continuously or all at once, are ingesting very large files, or have several simultaneous real-time feeds coming in, you will have capacity concerns and will likely need to work with the vendor to scale the solution to fit your needs.

Additionally, you need to be able to transcode audio and video upon export into appropriate editor formats. The system should automate this step so that users do not need to think about how to do it. This is part and parcel of streamlining the workflow and being able to do full digital round trips between the DAM system and the A/V editing environments. This implies that the DAM system supports "hot folders," which automatically ingest any A/V or other files it finds in that file system directory into the DAM system. Some systems that support round tripping may require customization; others already support it for Avid and FCP editing systems. Most DAMs already support hot folders. The system should also automatically distribute A/V files directly from the system to streaming servers, FTP sites, or other designated external outlets. While this isn't an absolute requirement, it can eliminate potentially repetitive manual work.

Because of the tightness of the A/V workflows and the requirements for transmitting large files among the DAM system, A/V editing suites, and reviewers, this scenario is typically implemented as an on-premise installation. If Web Services are supported for video editor integration, it can conceivably be developed in a SaaS model, but we would consider doing so a stretch. As mentioned previously, this scenario could be another shared use of the DAM system among many in your organization, especially if your organization has made a strategic commitment to digital infrastructure for the production, sharing, and distribution of digital assets. See Table 10.8 for further details.

TABLE 10.8 AUDIO AND VIDEO PRODUCTION AND REUSE

Information Model	Basic descriptive metadata as well as support for advanced A/V metadata extraction, presentation, and full-text search with indexing back to the video.
Workflows	• Deep video editing, including round tripping between DAM and A/V editing software • Deep integration with A/V editing tools • Material selection, review-approval A/V workflows • Basic file metadata workflows—extraction and later modification and annotation • Asset selection and grouping assets into projects • Clip selection and creation—rough-cut editing • Controlled workflows with check-in/check-out and revision control—add information over time, version A/V assets • Potential coordination with external workflow systems
Functional Emphasis	• Advanced A/V support with a focus on full support for A/V editing and rough-cut editing within the DAM system • Deep integration with A/V editing environments • Deep support for scalable A/V transcoding • A/V metadata extraction, scene detection, speech-to-text • A/V clip creation/rough-cut editing • A/V search and preview, support for storyboards • Security and access control supporting parallel workflows • Basic versioning • Ability to group and relate assets and projects • Ability to email links to assets • Web access and browser based • Installed
Typical Adopters	• Corporate communications • Corporate marketing • A/V production departments • Training organizations • Ad agencies • Media and entertainment companies
System Modifications	Advanced—Beyond the typical DAM setup (metadata/information model, users/roles/groups, security configuration), significant A/V workflow customization and integration typically are done by a vendor or one of its partners.

Broadcast Media Management

These scenarios are usually exclusively applicable to large media companies and broadcast companies. If you're in the business of creating television or streaming services, you'll also need very complex (and, unfortunately, expensive) technology to support it. If you're exclusively broadcasting on the Web, you may be able to just focus on the scenarios in the prior section.

Scenario 9: Television News

Producing a news broadcast is one of the most common broadcast-oriented DAM system use cases. Your news team works collaboratively with a production department or studio to produce audio and video for a television broadcast, but rather than passing video clips around via email or logging in to an FTP site to retrieve and view clips, you use the DAM system to share these files. You use the system to move, upload, store, review, annotate, and transfer clips and video works.

This scenario involves integration with audio- and video-editing functionality. Subsequently, the DAM system becomes a repository for audio and video files; it also helps manage the workflow among various team members. The system can store a combination of raw footage and final video clips.

In this workflow, the DAM system supports the following basic video capabilities and advanced broadcast capabilities:

- Upload video and audio files

- Enter detailed, layered metadata about the files

- Allow file versioning

- Make the files available to specific people on your team using the security model or the security model combined with shared folders

- Allow users to download and view files

- Allow users to make annotations to metadata or directly on videos for later review

- Use metadata to capture the approval status of the video and iterate through the workflow as needed

- Play the video or audio—most players support the ability to start at any point—and capture comments

Allowing for purely browser-based playback (rather than download and playback) is a nice feature. Note that this playback feature can add complexity to the back end because it requires a streaming server and additional storage for the streamed files.

For the simplest form of this scenario, you don't need advanced features like scene detection, speech-to-text, the ability to play from a specific time code (or frame) in a video, or clip creation features. These features add more editing capabilities, moving away from a simple review-and-approval process to a more powerful and complex A/V production and editing scenario.

Typical adopters of the technology for this scenario include major networks, major broadcasters, or large organizations that need to produce broadcast-quality video. See Table 10.9 for further details.

Scenario 10: Sports Broadcasting

Sports broadcasting is similar to news broadcasting, but more complex functionality is required to support the live/real-time demand of sports broadcasting. There are also more complex integrations required in sports broadcasting: immediate playback/instant replay and telestration play heavily in this scenario. *Telestration* is a host or operator drawing a freehand sketch over a moving or still video image (sometimes called an *electronic crayon*), which was popularized in the United States by John Madden. While this is a separate technology and not part of DAM functionality, there is often a requirement to use them both simultaneously.

Typical adopters of the technology for this scenario include TV sports networks, major broadcasters, and national and multinational sports organizations such as FIFA or the Olympics (see Table 10.10).

TABLE 10.9 TELEVISION NEWS

Core Functional Emphasis	• Emphasizes functionality to put together stories quickly
	• Availability of as much of the functionality via Web-based tools as possible, since news teams are remote and distributed
	• Integration with newsroom systems like NRCS, graphics, traffic, scheduling, and storage systems
	• Supports live ingest functionality, including scheduled, unmonitored, and DVR-like recordings
	• Provides logging tools for live events, and annotation tools for stories with archival value
	• Automatic low-resolution proxy creation and key-frame extraction from high-resolution video copies
	• Rapid search and retrieval
	• Low-resolution proxy browse, storyboarding tools, and edit decision list (EDL) export to nonlinear editing tools
	• Automated and background file transfers
	• Integration with many third-party devices such as
	• Video servers, production systems, and tape decks (including but not limited to GVG Profile, Sony XDCAM/ XDCART, Omneon Spectrum/Mediadeck, Imagine Communications Nexio, and DVW-500 VTRs)
	• Transcoding/conversion engines (such as Anystream Agility, FlipFactory, and Carbon Coder)
	• Archive Management Systems (such as DIVArchive, SGL FlashNet, and IBM Admira)
	Newer Areas
	• Ingest of content from mobile devices, particularly from reporters, citizen journalists, and eyewitnesses
	• Integrations with social networks such as Twitter and Facebook
	• Content publishing to Web and mobile platforms
Additional Considerations	• Users include journalists, editors, and producers
	• "Time to air" is of utmost importance
	• Workflows are story-centric

TABLE 10.10 SPORTS BROADCASTING

Core Functional Emphasis	• Requires functionality that supports the live nature of sports broadcasting
	• Supports the requirement to produce a highlights package of the event quickly
	• Metadata models for each sport exist and logging tools are custom built/prebuilt accordingly
	• Supports live ingest functionality, including scheduled, unmonitored, and DVR-like recordings
	• Provides logging tools for live events and annotation tools for stories with archival value
	• Automatic low-resolution proxy creation and key-frame extraction from high-resolution copies of videos
	• Rapid search and retrieval
	• Low-resolution proxy browse, storyboarding tools, and EDL export to nonlinear editing tools
	• Automated and background file transfers
	Newer Areas
	• Integrations with social networks such as Twitter and Facebook
	• Publishes lower-resolution video clips to Web and mobile platforms
Additional Considerations	With an eye on commercialization potential, sports channels maintain a large volume of archives, typically employing hierarchical storage management systems.

Scenario 11: Feature-Length TV and Cinema

Scenario 11 focuses on the production of long-form television programming and cinema, or even a long infomercial—anything longer than 30 minutes. From the infomercial to the TV program to the feature-length movie, the functional demands become increasingly complex.

A "digital daily" concept applies in this scenario and represents a snapshot of an in-process movie or video production work that's shared among the production team and corporate executives.

Typical adopters for this scenario include TV production houses, movie studios, and television stations (see Table 10.11).

TABLE 10.11 FEATURE-LENGTH TV AND CINEMA

Core Functional Emphasis	• The "Title" is the primary asset (that is, the feature/program itself)
	• Multiple supporting assets such as images, trailers, promotional materials, and multiple language audio tracks
	• Different workflows compared to news/sports broadcast:
	• Takes longer
	• Larger number of departments/teams involved
	• Giant amounts (sometimes thousands of hours) of raw footage
	• Typically involves integration with traditional enterprise systems such as finance and accounting, and enterprise search
	• Licensing and rights management functionality is often sought by clients given the potential opportunities for content syndication. For example, reruns of shows such as *Friends* and *Seinfeld* are syndicated globally
	• Need to support content encryption and security when content is distributed
	• The expected life of the content is comparatively much longer
	• Increasingly published on the Web and mobile devices
Additional Considerations	• Typically, ingest from multiple devices is not needed
	• Logging, annotation tools, and needs are different
	• What's important are subtitles and captioning for different markets and metadata at the overall video level. Unlike the Sports scenario, second-by-second logging is less important
	• Emphasis is on speech-to-text rather than manual metadata entry (at the frame/scene level); for instance, integration with subtitling/closed-captioning software
	• Promotions/trailers need EDL functionality (for example, integration with subtitling/captioning software), but not as extensively as the news/sports scenarios need it

Scenario 12: Radio Broadcasting

The Radio Broadcasting scenario focuses completely on audio production and broadcasting, and it is relatively simple compared to the prior scenarios. Typical adopters include radio stations and companies that produce podcasts or other online radio broadcasts (see Table 10.12).

TABLE 10.12   RADIO BROADCASTING

Core Functional Emphasis	• Ingest (feeds, wire agencies), news scripting, editing, review/approval, and (of course) metadata and search tools • Search, playlist creation, and editing/mixing tools • Requires content repurposing for podcasts/Web • Streaming and delivery through not only FM/AM, but also digital formats like HD Radio (for example, for delivery to Sirius XM Radio), with monetization through those additional channels
Additional Considerations	• Radio workflows differ from TV and may not be as complex, but they often require multiple, geographically disparate contributors to work together on program content/stories • Storage requirements are smaller and storage management is simpler because hierarchical storage management systems generally are not deployed

Scenario 13: Media Modernization and Archives

In addition to media companies, many different types of organizations—such as colleges, universities, national archives, museums, sports clubs and bodies, and others—have video collections or video libraries that may or may not be high definition (scenarios 9–11 typically involve HD). This scenario is applicable to any organization that needs to manage a video repository.

"Media modernization" is a conversion from analog formats (such as tapes) to digital formats. In this scenario, the terms *archives* and *collections* refer to a set of these digital multimedia assets. Assets in the archive may have been "born digital" or may have been modernized.

These assets may be at the end of a creative process, may be older, or may be used infrequently. The archive becomes a reference for historical asset use, regulatory compliance, a generator of new ideas (for example, using a nostalgic commercial in the new 50th anniversary campaign), scene re-creation, or a "reference library" (such as ad reels from 100 years of automotive manufacturing). They provide a rich source of insight and ideas for design work.

In essence, this scenario sets forth the notion of a single definitive catalog to display what the organization owns, as shown in Table 10.13.

TABLE 10.13   MEDIA MODERNIZATION AND ARCHIVES

Core Functional Emphasis	• Common functionality required includes search, browse, and annotations for metadata
	• Depending on the size of the archive, a separate storage management solution may be used
	• Depending on the intended use of the archive, integration with a licensing and rights management solution may be needed
	• Depending on the chosen delivery format, integration with transcoding software may be required
	• Depending on how new assets are added to the archives, an ingest module may be needed
Additional Considerations	• There is a distinction between the "Corporate Video" use case and this "Archives" use case because the integration with other enterprise systems is a key focus area for Corporate Video scenarios
	• Note that the news/sports archives of media companies are intended for different usage; subclips/parts of videos are often used in a story, but for the "Archives" use case, videos are typically consumed in whole or licensed out to others

Scenario 14: Parliaments, Government, Military, and Judicial

Parliaments and other legislative bodies are usually required to maintain records of their proceedings and make them available to the public or the media for future reference. Many of them even have dedicated channels to broadcast proceedings, such as C-SPAN's broadcasts of the US Congress. Usually, the video/audio archives are available for reference in the parliament library or on the Web.

Military and security DAM applications have a slightly more complex set of functions, and they focus less on archiving. The software often monitors a building or a geographic area, detecting movement and geotagging anything that's relevant. If nothing happens in the monitored video (for example, no one breaks in to the building or walks past the bolted door), it is discarded automatically. See Table 10.14 for further details.

TABLE 10.14 PARLIAMENTS, MILITARY, GOVERNMENT, AND JUDICIAL

Core Functional Emphasis	• Logging of proceedings with metadata annotation
	• Browse, search, and publishing to the Web are commonly required features
	• In many countries, multilingual support is required
	• Use cases for military and law-enforcement agencies are specialized and typically involve pattern recognition and/or monitoring of live feeds

Peripheral/Other Media Asset Management Use Case Scenarios

We haven't covered every possible media format and use case scenario, although we have covered the most widely used scenarios. As with any aspect of information technology, the industry and capabilities are constantly evolving. Tools and new markets are emerging that focus on specific media management scenarios, such as the following:

- **Long-Form Web Video:** Media companies are beginning to produce long-form video exclusively for the Web and mobile devices. This is happening particularly where video is tied to underwritten tie-ins such as Hearst with Fashion Week, so you might have 30-minute, designer interviews and mainline ads interspersed with an hour-long program. Unlike traditional productions, long-form web videos are rarely produced in high definition.

- **Specialized Classes of Science or Clinical Video:** In this use case, high-speed instrumentation imagery is used for medical— and even otherworldly (astronomic)—study.

- **Specialized Tools for Managing Gaming Assets:** Today the gaming production process is often more complex than creating a three-hour Oscar-worthy movie. Most gaming companies have developed bespoke managing methods that more resemble software development management than media management. DAM has yet to find a place in this process, but the rapid adoption of DAM systems to manage brand and image assets has gaming companies considering the alternatives.

- **E-Learning:** This is an entirely separate market of highly specialized tools that we have not covered in this book.

CHAPTER 11

Mixology: DAM in the Digital Marketing Cocktail

A book about DAM would not be complete without putting DAM in the bigger picture, and by that I mean the bigger picture of marketing technology. A DAM by itself has limited usefulness—those assets have to be pushed out and used by different technologies in a wealth of ways for all this effort to benefit your organization.

Although DAM historically was implemented in a silo, used and maintained by only a few marketers or archivists, that's changed. As mentioned in the introduction, DAM is now fully embraced by the C-suite as a key enterprise application. Just as much effort is being put into DAM systems connecting to other systems as deploying simply the DAM itself.

So how does DAM fit into the bigger picture of consumer-centric digital marketing? It's not always obvious. Choosing the right tools for holistic and effective digital marketing is not unlike crafting a complex cocktail: you have to find the right mix of ingredients and the right balance that works for you. What works for one organization might not work for yours, much like one person prefers a martini and someone else will prefer a negroni. Both drinks contain vermouth, just like two organizations might both have DAMs, but it's the mixing with the other ingredients that makes the results quite different and the right mix for you.

As a DAM practitioner or digital marketer, you need to think of yourself as the enterprise technology mixologist and work with your colleagues to come up with the right mix. So while DAM is obviously on your ingredient list, it's equally important to plan for the others and to understand the role that each technology plays. Otherwise, your cocktail will be no good, and no one will come back to your bar.

Here are a few things for you to consider as you work with your colleagues to weave DAM into the enterprise digital marketing cocktail:

- There are two digital marketing frameworks highlighted in this chapter that complement each other to help you chart the course for digital marketing effectiveness.

- A reference architecture built on foundations of customer- and product-centric data models can surface key gaps in systems and standards, and distinguish business services from business platforms.

- A consumer-centric reference model aligns enterprise-marketing investments with actual marketer and consumer needs.

DAM in a Digital Marketing Framework

The term "digital marketing technology" (or "MarTech" for short) has entered into common usage, although people often disagree on exactly what it means. Construed very broadly, digital marketing technology is the collection/cocktail of digital systems that marketers use to gather, cultivate, and nurture leads and customers. Traditionally, these systems reflected how a marketer wanted to represent a brand or product line. However, as marketing becomes (or aspires to become) more customer-centric, marketers increasingly sense that new approaches must focus much more intensely on customer preferences—including their browsing and buying history—and meet them in the channel of their choosing (mobile, in-store, catalog, or otherwise). Digital assets are instrumental for realizing this plan.

Top-performing organizations already recognize that a superior customer experience is intrinsically tied to the quality of their digital channels, and companies that sell tangible products effectively tie together in-store and digital shopping experiences. However, the quest for effectiveness in omni-channel marketing is hampered by a lack of practical frameworks to assess current states, conduct multi-stakeholder analysis, and help charter custom roadmaps for enterprise contexts.

In this regard, traditional IT-oriented architectural reference models can provide a layered inventory of digital marketing systems and provide a baseline for further analysis of functional (i.e., business), integration, and security/privacy needs.

However, a complementary approach to digital marketing as a strategy, practice, and technology examines the efficacy and usability of marketing systems *from the perspective of the customer.* A customer-centric reference model can more closely tie systems analysis to business value via the pursuit of brand awareness, customer engagement, and increased sales.

This chapter examines both types of reference models—enterprise-oriented as well as customer-centric—and offers advice on filling DAM into the bigger picture, seeking to systemically improve the effectiveness of their omni-channel marketing.

Reference Enterprise Architecture

The optimal enterprise digital marketing architecture can be usefully represented as a series of technology layers, from bottom to top (see Figure 11.1).

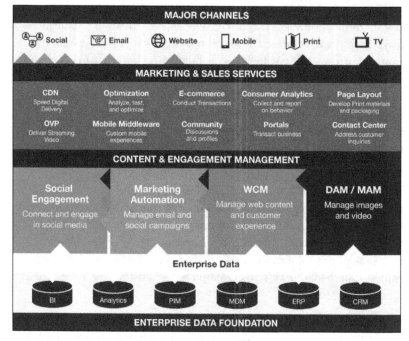

FIGURE 11.1

A traditional omni-channel marketing architecture reference model looks at systems in terms of layers—from the enterprise back-end forward to the frontline screen.

- **Enterprise data foundation:** Master product and customer data, analytics, and business intelligence. This might also include metadata you need to associate with the assets in your DAM.

- **Major marketing technology platforms:** Marketing automation, digital asset management, web content management, and social media engagement to manage content and engagement. Note, the colors of the arrows are quite deliberate here—the purple arrows show how the DAM's assets feed into other downstream marketing platforms.

- **Prototypical marketing and sales services:** E-commerce, self-service applications, online video platforms, and content delivery networks, which are often all using digital assets in some form. The DAM often transforms assets into the appropriate format, size and resolution for these services to deploy.

- **Major channels:** Channels such as mobile devices, websites, and kiosks—these are the "presentation layers," or "touch points" through which consumers access marketing and sales services. This is when the asset finally reaches the consumer.

Key Benefits

This approach represents an enterprise-centric view of digital marketing, one where DAM fits into a larger picture. Crucially, it takes a data-centric approach. Employ this type of reference model when:

- Determining how your DAM will interact with other enterprise systems: where it will pull data from and push assets to

- Holding discussions among disparate stakeholders, and you need to refer to a common set of terms and relationships

- Performing a rapid inventory of your key systems and frameworks; for example, you may be missing a consumer analytics tool or a product information management system—this will also influence your ability to measure the effectiveness of your assets

- Performing a "stoplight" analysis of where the enterprise is doing well or poorly; for example, you may be "green" in DAM, but only "red" in marketing automation and "yellow" in social engagement

- Distinguishing back-end data and content from the front-end user experience, and distinguishing marketing & sales services from underlying platforms (like DAM)

Customer-Centered Reference Model

A customer-centric model puts the customer at the center of the marketing technology strategy. You'll note that DAM is just a small part of this bigger picture, as shown in Figure 11.2.

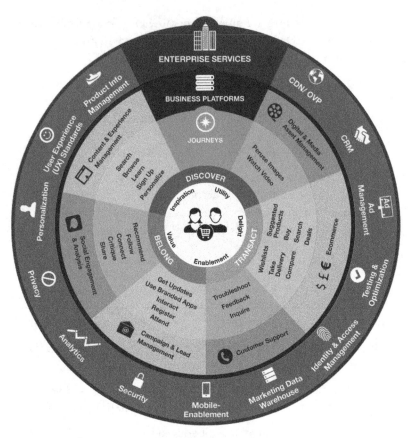

FIGURE 11.2

A customer-centered model puts the consumer/customer experience at the center, and it outlines layers of capabilities required to engage prospects and customers, creating more value for them and your company.

A key assumption here is that marketers' efforts to better engage consumers or increase consumer loyalty are a win-win for both parties. Consumers *want* to engage with brands, products, and services that are relevant to them; however, too often they struggle with digital experiences that frustrate this goal. Increased engagement results from explicitly shaping systems to address consumer needs and user experience—not just enterprise requirements. At the same time, consumer engagement must balance enterprise capabilities and concerns with consumer needs.

A consumer-centered approach offers several benefits:

- **It focuses your team.** By making the consumer the subject of the equation, it supports better alignment of enterprise investments with actual consumer needs and desires. Remember you're not buying a DAM for the sake of DAM—you're buying it because you have a customer need to fulfill.

- **It clarifies the distinction between platforms (gray) and applications (purple).** This distinction enables the enterprise to clearly separate roles and responsibilities, such that IT can own platforms, while business stakeholders can own specific applications.

- **It lends itself to "RACI" models where you can assign Responsible/Accountable/Consulted/Informed participation within a responsibilities matrix.** You can align your enterprise to be more agile and responsive to consumer needs.

- **It germinates discussion of personas and tasks.** These are the two essential building blocks for effective digital experiences.

Why These Models Are Important

By reading this book, you've invested quite a bit of time in learning about digital asset management technology. But don't forget, DAM is part of a cocktail. Marketing teams should work to expand their remit beyond just DAM, website management, or email automation toward a more integrated digital marketing experience.

Like all reference models, use these as a common frame for internal communications and alignment. At a minimum, employ these models to inventory your current environment and self-assess the effectiveness of it. Marketing leaders can use these models in several ways to simply drive stakes into the ground, take stock, or set signposts for strategy.

Finally, note that these models are deliberately succinct, and you may need to revise them for your own context.

Enjoy your time behind the bar!

INDEX

P

parallel workflow, 101–102

parliaments, government, military, and judicial, 202

partnerships and integration, 158–159

People category (DAM Maturity Model), 46–51

per-CPU licensing/pricing, 31

performance and scalability, 130–131

periodical and catalog production and management, 179–183

personalization

brand-based customization, 114

preferences-based, 113

role-based, 113–114

per-user licensing/pricing, 31

photo archive, 167–169

pointers, to remote files, 63

Portfolio NetPublish, 103

power user pricing model, 32

preferences-based personalization, 113

Prevalence dimension (DAM Maturity Model), 53–54

print ads, 174–175

private cloud service, 147

Processes category (DAM Maturity Model), 46–47, 56–57

professional services organization (PSO), 156–157

prototypical marketing and sales service, 209

proxy creation, 73

PSO (professional services organization), 156–157

public cloud service, 147

publishing

and DAM vendor evolution, 4–5

multichannel publishing scenario, 184–187

periodical and catalog production and management scenario, 179–183

R

RACI models, 211

radio broadcasting, 201

RealScore application, 46

reference enterprise architecture, digital marketing, 208–209

related assets, 86

rendering media processing capabilities, 74

rendition management, 14, 125

reporting and analytics, 122–123

Representational State Transfer (REST), 141–142

REST (Representational State Transfer), 141–142

reusable workflow, 102

Reuse dimension (DAM Maturity Model), 50, 52

revenue generation, 24–25, 28

rich media

challenges, 7–9

search, 91

risk mitigation, 28

roles and groups, system security, 118–120

roles-based personalization, 113–114

S

SaaS service, 148

SAN (storage area networks), 152

saved searches, 92

scalability and capacity, 123–126, 170

scalability and performance, 130–131

support, vendor
  community strength, 160
  documentation, 161
  factors affecting support, 159–160
system administration and application
  development, 116
system justification and expansion, 28
system modifications
  advertising and marketing asset
    management, 178
  audio and video library review and
    approval, 191
  audio and video production
    reuse, 195
  brand-centric asset management, 171
  DAM library or photo archive, 169
  multichannel publishing, 187
  multilingual brand management, 173
  periodical and catalog production and
    management, 183
Systems category (DAM Maturity
  Model), 46–47, 53–56

T

tagging, taxonomy management, 80
taxonomy management
  asset relationships, 84
  automated metadata extraction, 83
  community tagging, 80
  compound assets, 84–85
  configurations, 86–87
  dynamic schema support, 80
  findability, 77
  grouping assets, 81–82
  implicit and explicit metadata, 82
  information model
    establishment, 77–78
  metadata, controlled vocabulary, and
    schema support, 76–77

metadata definition and organization
  capabilities, 78–80
related assets, 86
schema change, 87–88
thesaurus functionality, 82–83
Technical Expertise dimension (DAM
  Maturity Model), 48
technology platforms, digital
  marketing, 208–209
technology services, DAM, 14–15
telestration, 197
television news, 196–198
thesaurus functionality, 82–83
time constraints, workflow feature, 102
training costs, 43
transcoding and transformation
  automated asset preparation, 108
  compound asset assembly, 110
  DRM encryption, 111
  file compression, 111
  image-rendering support, 109
  metadata export and
    transformation, 111
  metadata insertion or write-back, 111
  on-the-fly conversions, 108–109
  watermarking, 110
transcoding media processing
  capabilities, 74
transformation media processing
  capabilities, 74

U

UDDI standards, 141
UDP (User Datagram Protocol), 38
Usability dimension (DAM Maturity
  Model), 53–54
Use Cases dimension (DAM Maturity
  Model), 50–51, 53
User Datagram Protocol (UDP), 38

ACKNOWLEDGMENTS

There are countless people who have patiently taught, inspired, challenged, and pushed me in my career to be better at what I do, but in particular I would like to thank: my family, Margaret Heffernan, Grant Farrow, Howard Kogan, Laura Taylor, Anthony Wilson, Philip Wisniewski, Ralph Folz, Tony Byrne, Jarrod Gingras, and Mark Davey.

I am also grateful for the intellectual input from Joshua Duhl, Kashyap Kompella, Apoorv Durga, and David Lipsey that went into the early versions of the content that evolved into this book. Finally, thank you to Patricia Connelly and the team at Henry Stewart Events, for their tireless work on the annual DAM conferences in New York, Chicago, Los Angeles, and London, which form the foundation for our DAM community.

ABOUT THE AUTHOR

 Theresa Regli is a principal analyst and managing partner with the Real Story Group, covering and advising on digital and marketing asset management, marketing automation, creative operations management, and Web content management.

As a journalist in Boston in the early 1990s, Theresa first saw the Mosaic Web browser and was handed a 26-page book called "complete HTML" by her older brother, who offhandedly mentioned she'd probably end up working on "this thing called the Web" sometime in the future. She soon shifted from writing about the local arts scene to profiling new technologies and Internet start-ups, and then started coding.

After hand-coding one of the world's first newspaper websites amidst resistance from her paper-loving co-workers, Theresa moved on to join the dot-com wave, leading website development and information architecture teams, using early versions of what would eventually be called *content management systems*. From 2001 to 2006, she led a content management team at a systems integration firm, heading up implementations of major WCM, enterprise search, and DAM products.

Since joining the Real Story Group in 2006, Theresa has covered a multitude of content technology markets, with a particular focus on digital and marketing asset management. She advises a multi-industry, worldwide customer base that has included Unilever, Christie's, Johnson & Johnson, Sesame Workshop, Novartis, Ubisoft, the British Museum, IKEA, Capital One, the Ad Council, Havas Worldwide, the Council on Foreign Relations, Net-a-Porter, the UK National Trust, Shell, and the US Library of Congress.

Now based in her native city of Philadelphia, U.S., Theresa spends much of her life on the road, particularly enjoying London, Paris, Strasbourg, New Zealand, major tennis tournaments, and British Airways. When not working with Real Story Group customers or teaching seminars at events throughout the world, she is usually cooking, seeking out the best local restaurant, taking a scenic walk, or enjoying a hand-crafted artisan cocktail.

VENDOR EVALUATION RESEARCH

Real Story GROUP
MAKE BETTER
TECHNOLOGY DECISIONS

The Digital and Marketing Asset Management research critically evaluates the strengths and weaknesses of 30+ digital & marketing asset management products.

Digital & Marketing Asset Management

FIND OUT WHAT THE REAL INSIDERS KNOW

BECOME A HERO
- Get the inside scoop that will make you look smart
- Obtain external validation of your strategy and decisions
- Receive one-on-one help to solve your thorniest problems

SAVE TIME
- Get to a short list in minutes
- Get supporting artifacts to explain to your peers
- Transition to pilot projects faster

SAVE MONEY
- Learn how much these tools really cost
- Learn how to negotiate a better deal
- Learn about hidden costs and gotchas

ALIGN YOUR TEAM
- Obtain relevant education for business and IT stakeholders
- Get team-based workshops to put everyone on the same page
- Obtain a common vocabulary for how the tools really work

AVOID THE WRONG DECISION
- Learn the real story about vendor weaknesses to combat marketing hype
- Don't pick the wrong tool
- Discover a vendor you didn't know

For more information visit: www.realstorygroup.com

Printed in the USA
CPSIA information can be obtained
at www.ICGtesting.com
JSHW011518221024
72172JS00007B/54

9 781933 820729